Break Free of Chains

Break Free of Chains
How to Help Your Child Recover from Pornography Addiction

Christopher Bueker

Copyright © 2021 Christopher Bueker

All rights reserved.

No part of this publication may be reproduced, distributed, or transmitted in any form or by any means, including photocopying, recording, or other electronic or mechanical methods, without the prior written permission of the publisher, except in the case of brief quotations embodied in critical reviews and certain other noncommercial uses permitted by copyright law. For permission requests, write to the publisher, addressed "Attention: Permissions Coordinator," at the address below.

ISBN: 978-1-7371370-0-9 (KDP Paperback)

ISBN: 978-1-7371370-1-6 (KDP ebook)

ISBN: 978-1-7371370-2-3 (IngramSpark Paperback)

Library of Congress Control Number:

Printed by Christopher Bueker in the United States of America.

Interior design by Muhammad Imran.

Cover design by Muhammad Imran.

First printing edition 2021.

https://ChristopherBueker.com

Dedication

This book is dedicated to all people who struggle with addiction.

Contents

Dedication   v

Introduction   1
   The Purpose of This Book   5
   Who is This Book Written For?   6

Chapter 1: Recovery is Achievable   13
   People Do Recover from Addiction   13
   Understanding the Situation   19
   The Pornography Industry and Human Trafficking   22
   Sex Positivism and Feminism   32
   Abstinence and Harm Reduction   34

Chapter 2: Addiction and Internet Pornography   39
   Dependency and Addiction   39
   Symptomology and Pornography Addiction   45
   Why is Internet Pornography Addictive?   51
   Harms Associated with Internet Pornography Use   57

Chapter 3: Recovery and Authoritative Parenting   69
   What is Recovery?   69
   Authoritative Parenting   74

Chapter 4: Build a Foundation for Recovery   91
   Be Kind to Yourself   93
   Wise Up   95
   The Power of Your Subconscious Mind   101
   Spend Quality Time   107
   Educate Your Child   109
   Honesty, Accountability, and Motivation   112
   Listen and Then Discuss   116

Chapter 5: Take Action for Recovery   121
   Authoritative Parenting   121
   Identify Triggers   121
   Utilize Coping Skills   123
   Be A Benevolent Ruler   132
   Hold Your Child Accountable   142
   Reward Your Child for Appropriate Behavior   143
   Surrender and Let Go   149

Chapter 6: Maintain Long-Term Recovery   155
   Be Mindful of Substitute Addictions   157
   Positive Core Values   159

Live for the Why	164
Emphasize Giving Back	166
Continue to Intermittently Reinforce	168
Chapter 7: A Society Free from Addiction	**171**
Parent with the End Goal in Mind	171

Introduction

Even though I hold a license in the state of Ohio to practice chemical dependency counseling, please use this book at your discretion. Purchasing, reading, and implementing the strategies described in this book are not a substitute for professional treatment. Problematic use of internet pornography can be a serious matter and often calls for the care and treatment of a trained and licensed mental health therapist, psychologist, or treatment team.

Hello, parent of a child who has problematic use of internet pornography. My name is Christopher Bueker, and since 2015, I have provided individual and group therapy in the field of chemical dependency. I can relate to the pain that you are in. I have walked-the-walk in addiction recovery. These days, I counsel patients diagnosed with Substance Use Disorder; most, probably all of my patients are also diagnosed with another mental health condition. Most of my experience has been with medication-assisted treatment centers where I provide counseling services for patients diagnosed with Opioid Use Disorder. Over the years, I have gained much insight into addiction. Also, I have recovered from both substance abuse and pornography addiction.

I have professional training as a therapist, and I know addiction from personal experience as well. I have the best of both worlds if you will. Further, I see a void in the marketplace for such literature. Resulting from my expertise practicing as an addiction therapist, my recovery from substance abuse and internet pornography, and my training and practice of Yoga and meditation, I have written this guide to help parents who have a child (particularly for those still living in the house) who regularly consumes internet pornography. I observe trends in the field of mental health and the marketplace; I have noticed that, until now, there was no in-depth literature for parents with an adolescent struggling with compulsive use of internet pornography.

When writing this guide, I have conducted extensive research on the harms associated with the regular use of internet pornography; and the harms are widely documented. As a therapist, I am also well versed in parenting approaches that can assist in the recovery process. I draw from my professional training, research, and personal insight to bring you this book. Currently, I provide individual therapy for patients diagnosed with Substance Use Disorder (SUD) at a private psychiatric and mental health clinic in West Chester, Ohio, which is in the Greater Cincinnati area; I also provide Yoga and meditation classes to our patients.

From what I remember, my childhood was really good; and I have a pretty good memory. When I reached the age of 16, things started to change with my family dynamic. Through the pain and suffering that I experienced as a late adolescent, I started experimenting with psychoactive substances. As I was experiencing more and more pain and suffering, my experimentation with drugs eventually devolved into abuse and psychological dependency. In retrospect, I realized that for many years, I was subconsciously attempting to cover up my emotional state; I did not know how to process my emotions, so I turned to a chemical escape to self-medicate.

Introduction

I had a significant relationship in my life from the age of 15 to 19, and suddenly that relationship dissolved. This devastated me. The loss I experienced fueled my use. My substance abuse had negative impacts on my finances, grades, and relationships with people that love me. I struggled for a few years with depression and substance abuse. During that time, I was able to earn my Bachelor of Science in Psychology and entered the workforce. With my undergraduate degree in my hand, I started working as an assistant teacher at Cincinnati Public Schools and started growing my in-person social network. Connecting with like-minded individuals was very beneficial to me in overcoming my substance abuse and internet pornography addiction. In November 2011, I started practicing Yoga, and at that point, I dedicated myself to practicing it daily. After practicing daily for a few months, I quickly found myself in a Yoga Teacher Training in Cincinnati, Ohio. My experience with the teacher training provided the connection that I needed to help me overcome my problem with substance use. With connections to heart-centered folks and through the daily practice of Yoga and meditation, my substance abuse quickly faded.

Even though I was able to overcome my abuse of alcohol and drugs, my addiction to internet pornography persisted, despite the awareness that my use of it was not in alignment with my Yoga practice. After years of Yoga and meditation, I still struggled with my addiction to internet pornography. After years of pornography dependency, in 2017, I started to recover from my pornography addiction. I was only able to recover from pornography addiction when I:

- Processed my trauma via Eye Movement Desensitization and Reprocessing
- Participated in the NoFap community
- Participated in a Twelve Step program, SLAA
- Kept in contact with my sponsor and NoFap accountability partner
- Surrendered to my higher power
- Learned how pornography is linked to human trafficking
- Learned how regular pornography consumption was detrimental to living my fullest life

I feel so blessed to have overcome pornography addiction. I felt a need to put my experience into the form of a book, so I can share my intimate knowledge of recovery from internet pornography addiction with you.

I am delighted to share with you my specialized knowledge of addiction and recovery. I want your child to be free of problematic use of pornography. I want your child to heal from whatever fuels their psychological dependency on internet pornography. I send blessings and love to all the families with a member struggling with pornography addiction. As I wish peace and freedom for all people and sentient beings who inhabit the Earth, this guide has been created out of love.

Why am I qualified to write this book?

Although I have a formal education, the most valuable knowledge that I have today was acquired via personal

Introduction

experience. Perhaps, if you are wondering if I am qualified to write this kind of book, here are the reasons:

- Since 2015, I have been successfully practicing in the field of chemical dependency.
- I have helped many patients recover from opioid dependency.
- Since 2012, I have been practicing and teaching Yoga.
- I have recovered from drug abuse and pornography addiction.
- I have formal training in Psychology, behavioral science, addiction counseling, and Yoga.
- I am well-versed in recovery, personal development, leadership, transpersonal psychology, therapy, meditation, mastery, and parenting.

Further, I live an intentional life. I am constantly looking for new ways to improve; I practice *kaizen*, the Japanese practice of continual improvement. Also, I practice non-attachment. One of the things that motivated me to write his book is that I realize my experience helps many people overcome addiction and become better people in life.

The Purpose of This Book

The purpose of this book is to serve as a guide that assists parents in helping their child recover from internet pornography. This book provides education to parents about the nature of abuse, dependence, and addiction. It includes a review that delves into the nature of pornography and addiction, the harms associated with its use, and recovery approaches conducive to overcoming pornography addiction.

This book intends to give parents the upper hand when talking to their child about harms associated with the chronic consumption of digital pornography; it also provides knowledge and awareness regarding recovery from pornography addiction, so you are in the best position to compassionately and non-judgmentally address your child's use of internet pornography. When addressing the topic, it is beneficial to you as a parent to be versed in the harms associated with the regular use of mainstream pornography. Reading this book will give you the perspective that you need to motivate your child to change their short-sighted ways.

The purpose of this book is to help parents (and caregivers) of adolescents struggling with compulsive use of internet pornography. It gives you the proper mindset, tools, and strategies to help your child overcome pornography dependency. Conclusively, the book provides a set of premises, actions, and strategies that will allow you to help your child overcome their pornography addiction.

Who is This Book Written For?

This book is written for parents of adolescents and young adults who compulsively consume internet pornography. It is dedicated to mothers and fathers whose child has been negatively impacted psychologically, socially, or physiologically by their habitual use of internet

Introduction

pornography. This book is also very beneficial to educators, therapists, school counselors, and coaches who work with adolescents exhibiting problems associated with the chronic use of pornography. This book can be utilized by any conscious adult responsible for the care or education of the youth. It is specifically designed for moms and dads (and perhaps grandparents) with a child whom they speculate regularly visits pornography sites. This book can also be used by parents who have evidence that their child visits pornography sites. This book is also designed for parents whose child has openly acknowledged that they have uncontrollable use of online pornography.

What will I receive from reading this book?

This book offers a lot. You will gain so much by implementing the steps that are described in this book. By reading and implementing the strategies detailed in the book, you:

- Receive hope and inspiration
- Receive education and an understanding of compulsive use and addiction
- Receive insight and perspective on the progressive nature of addiction
- Learn about the harmful effects of pornography
- Learn about the similarities and differences between abuse, dependency, and addiction
- Learn why pornography is addictive for a certain percentage of people that use it

- Learn what pornography addiction looks like
- Learn strategies to address your child's addiction to internet pornography
- Acquire language to intelligently discuss the harms associated with the modern pornography industry
- Learn the benefits associated with authoritative parenting
- Know the importance of having house rules and following through with their implementation
- Learn about specific accountability software and the benefits of holding your child accountable for their internet behaviors
- Learn about the importance of core values and parenting with the end goal in mind
- Help visualize a society that is happy and free

Knowing about pornography, its commercialization, and human rights can be empowering; but, applying the knowledge *is* empowering. You must apply the knowledge, so your child can learn to use the internet for constructive purposes and recover from its destructive use. After reading this book, you realize that you are not alone in this matter. Other parents are in a similar situation; it is relieving to know that other parents are in your shoes. It is better knowing that you are not alone; that is why I created this book because I know many families have been harmed. Conclusively, the book is intended to provide an educational resource for you, including tools, skills, and perspectives about how to triumph over addiction.

Why is this book needed?

This book is needed for many reasons. A book like this does not exist yet, so there is a dire need for this literature. This book is also required because pornography addiction is on the rise and has been on the rise. In the United States, pornography is considered a public health crisis in 15 states.[1] This book is needed because it makes much more sense to put time, energy, and money into the prevention of pornography and internet addiction compared to it treatment. People struggling with addiction need help right now, but long-term, as a society, we need to be thinking about prevention. As of 2020, there is no available literature for parents to help their adolescent who is struggling with internet pornography use. This kind of guide is essential to society because it gives parents the tools to matter-of-factly address their child's problematic use of internet pornography.

This book has been published, so it functions as educational reference material and a how-to guide to assist your child in overcoming addiction to online pornography. The book is published because there is a need for it in society today. In recent years, therapists (such as myself) have been working with individuals struggling with compulsive internet pornography use; I know because my patients talk to me about the harms

---

[1] Lam, K. (2019, May 10). States call pornography a public health crisis; porn industry decries 'fear mongering'. Retrieved September 15, 2020, from https://www.usatoday.com/story/news/nation/2019/05/09/pornography-public-health-crisis-states-adopt-measures-against-porn/1159001001/

stemming from their use of it. This book exists to help with early intervention, so your child can minimize the damage they do. This book is published to serve as a useful and practical guide for parents and perhaps coaches, teachers, and mentors of adolescents who struggle with internet pornography use. The premises of this book include:

- People of all sexes and genders are created as equals.

- A percentage of people that use pornography become psychologically dependent on it.

- The compulsive use of pornography portraying sexual objectification is harmful psychologically, physically, and socially to both its users and those who are being objectified.

- Psychological dependency or addiction to internet pornography is a situation that needs to be addressed on a personal, familial, and societal level.

- Through motivation to change, accountability, and honesty, a recovery from compulsive use of internet pornography is achievable.

- You can assist your child, so it increases the likelihood that they will recover from their problematic use of internet pornography.

- By following the steps outlined in this book, your child can recover from their dependency on pornography.

Introduction

This book includes action steps that any parent can take to help their child recover from pornography addiction. As demonstrated, this kind of book is needed, and the content in it is valuable. In the upcoming chapters, the book focuses on the education of addiction, the construction of a foundation, and behavioral steps that can be taken to address your child's habit of using internet pornography.

Break Free of Chains

Chapter 1
Recovery is Achievable

People Do Recover from Addiction

Be optimistic. Look at things differently. Be hopeful that your child will recover because the good news is in. There is hope for your child who struggles with chronic use of internet pornography; you are reading this kind of book! That is amazing. Your child is much better off now. Many people have had worse addictions than compared to your child's habitual use of internet pornography. People recover from addiction by:

- Learning and using coping skills and relapse prevention strategies
- Learning to process their emotions
- Resolving any unprocessed suffering or trauma
- Developing a healthy in-person social network
- Changing their thoughts and beliefs
- Learning to delay gratification
- Engaging in constructive habits and living a healthy lifestyle
- Accepting non-judgmental accountability
- Identifying their core values and living a purposeful life

With the proper tools and guidance, your adolescent child can overcome their pornography addiction. With your guidance, accountability, and proper education about the seriousness of the matter, your child can learn to properly use the internet without succumbing to the temptation to engage in pornography use.

Today, there are more resources available to everyone around the world because of the internet. Dispensing of the internet altogether would be a major setback to virtually everyone, unless that person intends to live an ascetic lifestyle to reach enlightenment. For the general population, giving up the internet is not an option. It is almost like food and sex at this point. (That is a bit of an exaggeration; what I mean by that is, if you want to be successful in the world today, you most likely need reliable access to the worldwide web.) The internet is a force that we have to learn to work it. As conscious members of society, individuals have to learn to keep the internet in its place. With the information, education, and practical strategies that are provided in this book, your adolescent child can learn to keep their internet use in check and can learn to benefit from the internet, instead of allowing the internet to control them.

Literature delving into the recovery from internet pornography addiction is needed because of the high prevalence of compulsive pornography use by adolescences and adults alike. There needs to be prevention literature available for adolescents, families, and educators that instructs people on how to prevent addiction to social media, pornography, and the internet. More immediately, there is a need for literature that contains information about how to help a loved one overcome pornography addiction. This is where this book comes into play. This book is designed for parents and caregivers who have a child struggling with the use of internet pornography. You should be proud of yourself for seeking out resources that give you the tools you need to show your adolescent how to free themselves of pornography use. You are doing a good job by wanting to help your child.

This guide exists to help parents assist their child in overcoming pornography addiction. This book is designed to give parents tools and the language to help their child develop healthy coping skills, process any past suffering via therapy, and learn constructive ways of processing their emotions. This guide exists to help adolescents develop the proper skills they need to form and maintain healthy in-person relationships.

Addiction is about a lack of meaningful connection

Human beings are wired to bond and connect with themselves, each other, and the Earth. When we are happy, content, and healthy, we bond with the people that are around us. But suppose a person is unable to connect with people in their life because they are traumatized, isolated, or have been hurt by life. In that case, the individual becomes susceptible to bonding and connecting with something that offers a sense of relief. The unhealthy behavior that the individual engages in serves as a form of escapism. The unhealthy behavior could be mindlessly checking a smartphone, constantly using a street substance, playing video games, gambling, or compulsively using internet pornography.

Humans will bond with something because that is human nature, to connect and to bond. The path that frees oneself from an unhealthy bond is to make healthy connections, to be connected with people in the present moment. Addiction is just one side effect of the crisis of the disconnection that is happening in modern society.[2]

Understanding, compassion, emotional availability, accountability, and your child's buy-in are key in helping your child overcome their compulsive use of internet pornography. As stated, living in the past because of unprocessed suffering or being anxious about the future is one thing that makes an individual susceptible to compulsive use of drugs or internet pornography. Authoritative parenting aims to prevent addiction; yet, if addiction gets a grip of your child, following the steps outlined in this guide will give you the tools to compassionately and competently address and likely redirect your child's behavior in a different, positive direction. The remedy to addiction is connection, that is, connecting with friends, family, and community. Recovery from addiction also involves identifying values and living a purpose-driven life. Figuring out the why in life is critically important when recovering from habitual engagement in destructive behavior (as in process addiction) or compulsive use of psychoactive substances. (More to be discussed about process addiction in the upcoming chapters.)

Connection is the remedy for addiction

As stated, addiction is about the lack of meaningful connection in a person's life. Connection is the remedy for addiction, as connection is the opposite of addiction. There are many ways to experience connection. Many of these ways involve interacting with other people, as

---

[2] Kurzgesagt (Ed.). Addiction. Retrieved 2020, from
https://www.youtube.com/watch?v=C8AHODc6phg&t=38s

humans are social creatures. There are other ways to experience connection, which do not require interaction with other people. Interaction with other people is a great way to experience connection; yet, we have to develop alternative ways of experiencing connection that does not require other people's participation.

How much connection a person experiences in their life often is highly correlated to the happiness and feelings of self-worth that the individual experiences. Biologically, humans are wired for connection. Deep forms of connection that a person experiences in the world ultimately lead to a meaningful and purpose-driven life. If a person is disconnected, alone, or separated from the people around them, the individual increases the likelihood that they will develop compulsive destructive tendencies. Further, people struggling with addiction often experience loneliness. That is, part of the recovery process involves feeling and being connected. Recovery also involves forging connections to people, places, and things that contribute to the individual's life. To experience more connection in your everyday life, do the following:

- Be authentic
- Be mindful
- Maintain a positive attitude
- Express genuine interest in other people
- Serve yourself and other people
- Spend time in nature
- Minimize your time on electronic devices

- Practice compassion for yourself and others
- Embrace vulnerability
- Embrace your emotional nature
- Avoid viewing vulnerability as a weakness
- Avoid judging yourself and other people
- Forgive people who may have hurt you
- Apologize if you have hurt another person

You can also teach your child about experiencing more connections in their life. In the next section, you will learn about immersing yourself in the activity you are doing, connecting with the activity, becoming one with the activity.

What is flow state?

Flow or flow state refers to an optimal state of consciousness, where the individual is performing flawlessly. Experiencing flow generally refers to moments in time where the individual is absorbed in the task that they are doing. In the state of flow, action and awareness are present. The individual's sense of self, ie, their ego, takes a back seat, and the individual is functioning as one with the Universe. In a flow state, it feels as if the individual is becoming one with the task they are engaging in. When experiencing flow, some core characteristics emerge and the individual experiences:

- An interplay among action and awareness
- The ego taking a backseat or vanishing
- Significant distortion of time

- All aspects of mental and physical performance significantly increase

Flow or being in the zone represents "a mental state in which a person performing an activity is fully immersed in a feeling of energized focus, full involvement, and enjoyment in the process of the activity. In essence, flow is characterized by the complete absorption in what one does, and a resulting transformation in one's sense of time."[3]

When a person is experiencing flow state, they are connecting with the Universe. When a person has problematic substance use or a process addiction, the individual is rarely experiencing a flow state. When a person is experiencing flow consciousness, their bodily needs seem irrelevant. People experiencing flow can often go hours without eating food or even skip a meal because they are so present in the moment. People who are mired in their addiction are unable to access flow state because they are constantly focusing on what their body or mind needs. Further, recovery from addiction involves finding activities and situations that individuals can experience flow.

Understanding the Situation

What is pornography?

Pornography is the "portrayal of sexual subject matter for the exclusive purpose of sexual arousal."[4] According to The

---

[3] Flow (psychology). (2020, July 29). Retrieved August 08, 2020, from https://en.wikipedia.org/wiki/Flow_(psychology)

[4] Pornography. (2020, August 03). Retrieved August 08, 2020, from https://en.wikipedia.org/wiki/Pornography

University of Iowa, pornography is "printed or visual material containing the explicit description or display of sexual organs or activity, intended to stimulate erotic rather than aesthetic or emotional feelings."[5] Pornography:

- Is sexually explicit
- Includes images of sex organs or sexual acts that are unconcealed
- Is intended to incite sexual arousal.[6]

That is, pornography is the explicit depiction of sexual acts with the intent to stimulate sexual arousal. *Internet pornography* is pornographic material that is hosted online, generally as video content. Further, high-speed internet pornography is a whole another animal because it presents additional challenges that were not present through magazines and VHS forms of pornography. The ubiquitousness of internet pornography provides its own set of challenges for the addicted user. By reading this book and implementing the steps, you will help your child live a healthier life.

What is commercial sex?

Commercial sex is any sex act that is performed for the exchange of money or anything of value. Commercial sex has nothing to do with consensual sex; commercial sex is the opposite of free love. The United States Department

---

[5] Pornography. (2020). Retrieved August 25, 2020, from https://legal.studentlife.uiowa.edu/protect-your-future/pornography/

[6] McKee, A., Byron, P., Litsou, K., & Ingham, R. (2020). An interdisciplinary definition of pornography: Results from a global Delphi panel. *Archives of sexual behavior*, *49*(3), 1085-1091.

of State defines a commercial sex act as "any sex act on account of which anything of value is given to or received by any person."[7] On the surface, pornography performers are paid to appear in pornography. The definition of commercial sex certainly applies to the pornography industry. Forms of commercial sex include:

- Prostitution and brothels
- Pornography
- Webcam sex
- Stripping
- 'Massage parlors'[8]

Why am I talking about commercial sex in a guide that is designed to help you assist your child in overcoming their addiction to internet pornography? I mention this because once your child and you realize that the mainstream pornography industry is integrally linked to human trafficking, you can use this knowledge as a major motivating force to free your child from internet pornography. Further, *human trafficking* is the trade of human beings for the purposes of forced labor, sexual slavery, and commercial sexual exploitation for the trafficker; human trafficking is the illegal trade of people for commercial exploitation.

Pornography addiction is such a powerful force; to give your child the best opportunity to recover from

---

[7] Definitions of Human Trafficking. (2009). Retrieved August 08, 2020, from https://2001-2009.state.gov/g/tip/c16507.htm

[8] Farley, M. (2006). Prostitution, trafficking, and cultural amnesia: What we must not know in order to keep the business of sexual exploitation running smoothly. *Yale JL & Feminism, 18*, 109.

pornography addiction, your child needs to know that the pornography industry as a whole cannot be separated from sex trafficking. Knowing that when an individual increases the demand for commercial sex, they are directly or indirectly a contributing force that increases the supply of commercial sex, whether the involved sex performer gives consent or not.

The Pornography Industry and Human Trafficking

Regular use of misogynistic, mainstream pornography use is destructive in many ways. Pornography portraying the objectification of women is a perversion of human sexuality. Watching pornography portraying the objectification and debasement of women distorts the mind. Most mainstream forms of internet pornography show the objectification, commodification, and degradation of women. The portrayal of women as sex objects warps people's minds and distorts their views of sexuality; hardcore, mainstream pornography sexualizes all people, but more particularly women. The pornography industry shows women as merely sex objects. Mainstream pornography shows the picture: women are not to be treated like human beings; women are to be treated as sex objects - to be used and abused by men.

Mainstream pornography shows women getting slapped, spit on, and jerked around - only to be forcefully penetrated by angry-looking men. The bestselling pornography often portrays men calling women dirty names such as "whore, slut, bitch, etc." Many times when a woman is physically and verbally abused in films, the pornified woman's facial expression is neutral, or the female actor is putting on a fake smile.[9] This normalizes the abuse women experience in the production of mainstream pornography. In return, some adolescents and even adults, especially those dependent on internet pornography have a difficult time relating to humans of the opposite sex in real life because their minds have been conditioned through porn culture to view humans as merely sex objects.

I cannot say it better myself, so I yield to researchers and other advocates in the field. Here is what other leaders say about the harms associated with the pornography industry:

"Pornography is an act of prostitution. A survivor of prostitution explained, 'Pornography is prostitution that is legalized as long as someone gets to take pictures.' Pornography documents and facilitates trafficking... The real lives of those who are trafficked, prostituted, or made into pornography are often indistinguishable from the real lives of victims of rape, incest, and intimate partner violence. The main difference is money. Profits turn sexual assault of children, rape, domestic violence, humiliation, and sexual harassment, and pictures taken of those things - into a business enterprise."[10] ~Melissa Farley, American clinical psychologist, researcher, and feminist activist

---

[9] Whisnant, R. (2016). Pornography, humiliation, and consent. *Sexualization, Media, & Society*, *2*(3), 2374623816662876.

[10] Farley, M. (2015). What are the connections between prostitution, pornography, and sex trafficking? In J. Vanek (Author), The essential abolitionist: What you need to know about human trafficking & modern slavery. United States: Daliwal Press.

"There has always been pornography, but there has not always been a porn industry."[11] ~Gail Dines, leading academic expert on harms associated with mainstream pornography

"Women are lured in, coerced and forced to do sex acts they never agreed to do...[and given] drugs and alcohol to help [them] get through hardcore scenes.... The porn industry is modern-day slavery."[12] ~Shelley Lubben, a former pornography performer

"To make visual pornography, the bulk of the industry's products, real women and children, and some men are rented out for use in commercial sex acts."[13] ~Catharine MacKinnon, American legal scholar, feminist, activist, and author.

"While pornographic content includes trafficked victims from around the world, porn consumers aren't told anything about the performers, including which ones may have been trafficked from an early age. Regular users of internet pornography are likely consuming pornography that includes adult and child victims of sex trafficking."[14] ~Noel Bouché, Executive Director of pureHOPE

---

[11] Bindel, J. (2014, October 24). Without porn, the world would be a better place | Julie Bindel. Retrieved August 08, 2020, from https://www.theguardian.com/commentisfree/2014/oct/24/pornography-world-anti-porn-feminist-censorship-misogyny

[12] Bouché, N. J. (2009). Exploited: Sex Trafficking, Porn Culture, and a Call to a Lifestyle of Justice.

[13] MacKinnon, C. A. (2004). Pornography as trafficking. *Mich. J. Int'l L.*, *26*, 993.

[14] This Is How Porn And Sex Trafficking Are Linked - Be Part of The Solution. (2020, January 06). Retrieved August 03, 2020, from https://conquerseries.com/this-is-how-porn-and-sex-trafficking-are-linked/

These authors, researchers, and advocates authoritatively speak about how the pornography industry is integrally linked with human trafficking. If your loved one is consuming pornography that they gain access to via the internet, it is reasonable to conclude that your child is increasing the demand for commercial sex, which you have learned increases the demand for women in the commercial sex industry.

The video content that is "freely" available on tube-style pornography sites (PornHub, xVideos, xHamster, YouPorn) features a majority of pirated material. This is another layer of bad karma for the individual who uses pirated pornography. The pornography industry is all about stealing the vital life energy from the performers in the videos, particularly dehumanizing women, and suppressing the feminine. This has grave implications for people consuming pornography that portrays the objectification and degradation of women.

In the practice of Ashtanga Yoga, there are ten ethical standards that one has to adhere to achieve contentment and happiness. Ahimsa, brahmacharya, and asteya are three of these values. Ahimsa is the value that involves avoiding the harm of other sentient creatures. Brahmacharya is about honoring the vital life energy of other living creatures and yourself. Asteya is the value that involves non-stealing. All three of these values are violated when one is consuming pornography portraying the objectification and commodification of a woman or any person on that matter. Regularly using internet pornography, which is often associated with solo ejaculation, is corrosive to an individual's health and well-being. As any form of escapism is not conducive to a healthy lifestyle, people escaping through the use of drugs or pornography are not healthy people.

I am not saying that your child and you must adopt these values to help your child overcome addiction to internet pornography. At the same time, from my recovery and my professional experience as a successful addiction therapist, it is much easier for an individual or a family to recover from addiction when the user allows humanistic values to serve as their compass in life. Later on in this book, I will delve further into core values and living a purposeful life.

Descent human beings oppose human and sex trafficking, but they are unaware of how the consumption of misogynistic, mainstream pornography increases the demand for human trafficking. *Sex trafficking* is the force, coercion, or intimidation into sexual acts that go against the individual's will for commercial exploitation for the trafficker. The pornography industry and the commercial sex industry are intrinsically linked to human trafficking. There is a simple reason for this: supply and demand. When a person seeks out commercial sex whether it be through internet pornography or buying prostitution services, the demand is so high that the market cannot provide enough voluntary participants to the sex buyers. Therefore, the market is "forced" to coerce and intimidate women into the commercial sex industry.

This demand in pornography consumption cannot be met, so the market resorts to illegal means to supply the demand. There is a whole international movement that creates awareness for reducing and eliminating the demand for commercial sex. (Find more information at StopDemand.com and the National Center on Sexual Exploitation at EndSexualExplotation.org.) If you want to do your part and reduce the demand for commercial sex, teach your child about significantly reducing or eliminating internet pornography consumption.

If your child is psychologically dependent on the consumption of digital pornography, they have formed a dependency on it because of its anonymity, affordability, and accessibility. The pornography industry is responsible for this. The problem is how the pornography industry is manifesting itself in the world today. This book reviews the harms associated with the pornography industry. That is, scientific evidence shows that 88% of mainstream pornography consumed in the United States contains violence towards women.[15] More specifically, "of the 304 scenes in the movies, 88% contained physical violence, and 49% contained verbal aggression. On average, only one in 10 scenes do not contain any aggression, and the typical scene averaged 12 physical or verbal attacks."[16] In 2010, "researchers analyzed more than 300 porn scenes and found that 88% contained physical aggression. Most of the perpetrators were male, and their targets are female, and the latter's most common response to aggression was to show pleasure or respond neutrally."[17] As stated earlier,

---

[15] Bridges, A. J., Wosnitzer, R., Scharrer, E., Sun, C., & Liberman, R. (2010). Aggression and sexual behavior in best-selling pornography videos: A content analysis update. *Violence against women*, *16*(10), 1065-1085.

[16] How Porn is More Violently Dehumanizing and Sexually Objectifying to Women than Ever. (2020, February 20). Retrieved August 02, 2020, from https://fightthenewdrug.org/how-watching-porn-erodes-views-of-women/

[17] Is porn harmful? The evidence, the myths and the unknowns. (n.d.). Retrieved August 02, 2020, from

this normalizes the abuse that women experience. This is not acceptable in a free and open society.

"There are further undeniable links between pornography use and decreased sexual satisfaction, sexual function, relationship satisfaction, attraction to real-life partners, and acceptance of terribly dangerous myths about rape. Further, the pornography industry works hard to keep up a glamorous image, but behind the camera is a reality of violence, drugs, and human trafficking."[18] Further, pornography addiction did not surface in society to the degree that it has now until the pornography industry became so dominant in society. Pornography addiction has surfaced in society because digital pornographic content:

- Is accessible
- Can be viewed anonymously
- Is "affordable"

To avoid talking about the pornography industry's link to human trafficking in this kind of book would be neglectful; I would be remiss in my responsibilities by not including a bit on it.

In my practice of addiction counseling, I orient toward harm reduction and encourage abstinence from the destructive use of substances. "*Harm reduction*, or harm minimization, refers to a range of public health policies

---

https://www.bbc.com/future/article/20170926-is-porn-harmful-the-evidence-the-myths-and-the-unknowns

[18] Kite. (2017, October 11). Lessons from Porn: Women are Objects to be Used, Abused and Dismissed. Retrieved August 02, 2020, from https://beautyredefined.org/lessons-from-porn-women-are-objects/

designed to lessen the negative social and physical consequences associated with various human behaviors, both legal and illegal."[19] Harm reduction practices might be able to be implemented when assisting your child in overcoming their compulsive use of internet pornography.

The use of internet pornography is a slippery slope because of its addictive potential. I explain this in an upcoming chapter about how sex is a basic need, how sex is reinforcing, and how novel sexual experiences are rewarding. Because of all these features, I know that abstinence is the best for me. I cannot say what is best for your child. Also, I realize that other people may have experienced success in clearing up their problematic symptoms through harm reduction practices when recovering from pornography addiction. I am not necessarily advocating for abstinence, but I know that I can say for certain: abstinence from commercial sex will significantly increase the likelihood that your child experiences success in their personal, romantic, and professional endeavors.

One of the main goals of recovery is to reduce, manage, and potentially eliminate the mental health symptoms that are associated with problematic use. That is, addiction equals impairment. No impairment, no addiction. (Psychological dependency is a little bit different; I explain in the next chapter.) Often, people struggling with the chronic use of internet pornography minimize problems that originate from their dependency; the individual is experiencing denial. Many people deny

---

[19] Harm reduction. (2020, July 10). Retrieved August 06, 2020, from https://en.wikipedia.org/wiki/Harm_reduction

the reality that their uncontrollable use of internet pornography has detrimental effects on their minds and bodies. For individuals to overcome their denial, they need to be faced with compassion and non-judgment when talking about their problems.

How to reduce demand for commercial sex acts is a topic that transcends the nature and scope of this book. For this book, to reduce the demand for commercial sex, significantly reduce or stay abstinent from the use of internet pornography. In age-appropriate language, teach your child about the importance of reducing demand and hopefully eliminating the demand for commercial pornography. To find out more about how pornography and human trafficking are linked, read the following reports and journal articles:

- Pornography: Driving the Demand in International Sex Trafficking[20]

- Human Trafficking and Pornography: Using the Trafficking Victims Protection Act to Prosecute[21]

- Intersections between Pornography and Human Trafficking: Training Ideas and Implications[22]

---

[20] Guinn, D. E., & DiCaro, J. (Eds.). (2007). *Pornography: driving the demand in international sex trafficking*. Xlibris Corporation.

[21] Luzwick, A. J. (2017). Human trafficking and pornography: Using the Trafficking Victims Protection Act to prosecute trafficking for the production of Internet pornography. *Nw. UL Rev.*, *112*, 355.

[22] Humphreys, K., Le Clair, B., & Hicks, J. (2019). Intersections between Pornography and Human Trafficking: Training Ideas and Implications. *Journal of Counselor Practice*, *10*(1), 19-39.

- The Connection Between Sex Trafficking and Pornography[23]
- Pornography, prostitution and international sex trafficking: Mapping the Terrain[24]

You are not alone

As a parent of a child who compulsively uses internet pornography, you are not in this alone. The prevalence of internet pornography use is high. Many parents are in the same situation, where they have a child living at home that is addicted to internet pornography. Now more than ever, there are ways to connect with other parents via the internet, where you can discuss your child's addiction to internet pornography and support each other. Also, consider an in-person support group for yourself where you can talk to other parents who have an addicted loved one. There may be a support group in your area that is sympathetic to you being a parent who has a child addicted to internet pornography. Also, consider talking with a therapist about coping and dealing with this situation. This is designed as a self-help guide. At the same time, this guide is synergized by participation in individual therapy, if it is beneficial to you. As mentioned in the introduction, this book is not a substitute for professional help.

For some parents, on the one hand, realizing that their child has an addiction to internet pornography can be

---

[23] Lillie, M. (2014). The connection between sex trafficking and pornography. *Human Trafficking Search: The Global Resource and Database*.

[24] Guinn, D. E. (2006). Pornography, prostitution and international sex trafficking: Mapping the Terrain. *Available at SSRN 885389*.

devastating, and on the other hand, some parents realize that their child's addiction to internet pornography is just another challenge that they experience as parents. Acceptance of the situation is critical, so you can compassionately and non-judgmentally address the situation.

Sex Positivism and Feminism

Sex positivism is an attitude toward human sexuality that regards in-person sexual activities amongst consenting adults as fundamentally healthy and pleasurable; sex positivism also encourages sexual pleasure and experimentation solo or with a partner, as long as all involved are truly consenting. Further, the sex-positive movement is a social and philosophical movement that advocates these attitudes. The problem with the pornography industry is that some of the women performers and now men and young boys and girls appearing in it are not there of their free will or choice.

Mainstream pornography overwhelmingly objectifies women; and today's pornography industry is all about the debasement and hatred of women and the feminine. This is not good for the male or female or anyone's psyche. There are small pockets of independent pornography producers, which are owned and operated by women; this marginal sector of the market portrays female empowerment, women's sensuality, and women experiencing pleasure. This kind of adult art is very much neutral in their presentation, and these kinds of artisan pornography companies portray egalitarian roles shared by the performers who are having sex. This represents a very small niche sector of the overall pornography industry. This kind of pornography costs money to purchase and is not available on any tube-style pornography sites. This book is not referencing the aforementioned genre of adult entertainment.

This book mentions the commercialized pornography industry, which exploits and dominates women and the feminine for profit. There are massive market forces in the pornography industry that exploit and harm women and as such are harmful to society as a whole. There is no stepping around this. This is not a topic of debate. This is a reality of the world in which we live today. Further, some people try to reason for the legalization of commercial sex and equate the issue to that of the decriminalization and legalization of psychoactive drugs. In my opinion, the decriminalization and legalization of controlled substances have their merit, but some people often identifying as *liberal*, who advocate for commercial sex legalization, under the guise of feminism, seem to be unaware of the fact that women are not objects. A psychoactive substance, a drug is not a living being. Women are human beings.

In summary, *"feminism* is a range of social movements, political movements, and ideologies that aim to define, establish, and achieve the political, economic, personal, and social equality of the sexes."[25] That is, there is nothing feminist about pornography that portrays the objectification, commodification, and the degradation of women. Mainstream pornography, which most often depicts verbal abuse and physical assault of women is

---

[25] Beasley, C. (1999). What is feminism?: An introduction to feminist theory. Sage.

inherently anti-feminist and anti-human. Shedding light on the violence and trafficking associated with the commercial sex industry helps advocate for equality among men, women, and people of all sexes and genders. Conclusively, a person can be sex-positive and feminist and still abstain from the consumption of internet pornography.

Abstinence and Harm Reduction

The lower a person's rock bottom, the more the person will benefit from choosing abstinence from pornography use. On the one hand, *abstinence* is the practice of avoiding use altogether; abstinence is a form of restraint from indulging in the act of consuming pornography. On the other hand, harm reduction is a practice that intends to significantly decrease harms associated with risky behaviors. Often, abstinence is the best choice for those recovering from a serious addiction problem.

The lower a person's rock bottom, the more important it is for the recovering individual to adhere to abstinence. That is, the worse the addiction is, the more harm that is created in the individual's life. If a person's addiction has severely impacted the individual's health and well-being, they will greatly benefit from practicing abstinence. Once a person is addicted to a substance or a process, the neural networks have already been primed for addiction to come back much more quickly. That is, once the neural networks in the individual's brain have formed and then dwindled, their potential reformation comes about much more quickly. For recovery to occur, the individual will have to learn how to do different behaviors that utilize the

Addiction and Internet Pornography

other neural networks, which allow the person to feel good naturally.

Once these new pathways are created, the old neural pathways, which were highly myelinated from the person doing the behavior over and over again, start to die away. The superconductivity of those neural networks falls apart when the person learns new constructive ways of making themself feel good naturally. Suppose your child has a severe form of pornography addiction, I believe they put themselves in the best position for personal and professional success through abstinence from pornography.

If your child has not undergone major negative impacts but would still like to reduce their use of internet pornography, your child might be able to take a more of a harm reduction approach to recovery. In cases where the individual has undergone major negative consequences resulting from their chronic use of internet pornography, the individual maximizes their opportunity for long-term success by adhering to abstinence. The following are harm reduction approaches to pornography addiction. If your loved one is going to use, these steps can be taken to reduce the risks of chronic use of internet pornography.

- Only view pornography that is paid for
- Only view pornography casting performers with a net worth greater than a million dollars
- Only view pornography after all the chores and projects are complete for the day and week

- Track the amount of time that is spent viewing pornography and discuss with an accountability partner
- Track the kind of pornography that is being viewed
- Journal what it felt like to relapse and use pornography
- Avoid the use of tube-style and other forms of pirated material
- Avoid consumption of pornography portraying sexual objectification
- Use accountability software
- Participate in the NoFap or Twelve Steps fellowship program
- Engage in individual or group therapy

The problem with pornography is that it is so addictive. Some researchers in the field refer to pornography as "digital heroin."[26] Theoretically, one might be able to apply harm reduction principles to recover from internet pornography addiction; but, I honestly do not see it as a viable path. The choice is yours.

In this chapter, you learned:

---

[26] DiPietrantonio, S. (2017, November 06). Porn and smartphones: 'We don't realize how dangerous it is,' expert says. Retrieved August 23, 2020, from https://www.fox19.com/story/36777429/porn-and-smartphones-we-dont-realize-how-dangerous-it-is-expert-says/

- Through motivation, honesty, accountability, awareness, and connection, your child will be able to recover from pornography addiction.
- Addiction occurs when an individual goes without meaningful connection in their life; the individual then develops an unhealthy connection with their choice of addictive act.
- Connection with oneself, other people, and a higher power is the remedy for addiction.
- Pornography is an explicit depiction of sexual acts with the intended purpose of arousal.
- Commercial sex is any sexual act that is traded for something of economic value, ie money or drugs.
- The pornography industry is linked to sex trafficking because the commercial sex industry cannot meet the demands of the market and thus resorts to illegal forms of trafficking to supply the market demand.
- Sex positivism is the view that sexual activity among truly consenting adults is a natural and healthy aspect of the human experience.
- Feminism is the view that people of all sexes and genders are equal in society.
- Abstinence involves the complete avoidance of the substance or behavior; harm reduction is an approach that seeks to minimize the harm associated with risky behaviors

.

Break Free of Chains

Chapter 2
Addiction and Internet Pornography

Dependency and Addiction

What is a habit?

A *habit* is a behavior that a person does over and over again without conscious input. A person forms certain habits, and they tend to continue throughout the person's lifetime. In psychology, a habit represents a static way of thinking or feeling through the repetition of a mental experience.

People can form positive and negative habits. People more often than not, do not notice their habits, but they may notice other people's habits and sometimes find them to be off-putting. Positive habits lead to success in personal and professional endeavors; yet, negative habits can lead to a lifelong struggle with compulsive use of a substance or a process behavior and other mental health symptoms. Sometimes, a person puts conscious thought into their habitual behaviors; more often, the person does not put conscious thought into them.

A habit is a pattern of behavior that occurs regularly and its operation tends to occur on a subconscious level. Further, people's habits work in a particular way. First, there is a catalyst or a stimulus that puts the behavior in motion, which is the *antecedent*. Second, the catalyst triggers a routine. Third, there is the payoff; there is a reward that the individual is seeking. The three steps of a habit include:

1. The antecedent, the trigger, the cue
2. The routine of the behavior, the use of pornography
3. The reward, the payoff, what the individual gets out of the behavior

A lot of times a person using compulsively does so because they are attempting to cover up their emotional state. The use of substances and process addictions do not cover up the emotional state of the individual who uses, but simply dampens the suffering that the individual is experiencing. The process of engaging in habitual behavior such as drug use or paired masturbation and pornography use generally compounds the user's problems.

Abuse is any use of a substance or process behaviors (such as pornography use) that leads to negative consequences. Abuse can be one of two things or a combination of both, binge use or habitual use that leads to negative consequences. Binge use refers to excessive use in a single session. Habitual use occurs regularly; often, regular consumption of a drug or of internet pornography manifests itself as daily use. Often, abuse is both binge and daily use, which enters into the territory of dependency and addiction.

Example 1. The guy who goes out with his old college friends once a year and drinks 6 beers in a two-hour session. This person barely drinks throughout the year yet feels obligated to throw back a few beers to remember the good days, which are reminiscent of his time in college when he used to get intoxicated with his college buddies.

In this example, the guy is abusing alcohol once a year but otherwise does not have a dependency or addiction to alcohol.

Example 2. The person who smokes cigarettes every day. The person can function in everyday society yet experiences some negative consequences such as coughing and susceptibility to lung cancer. In this example, nicotine abuse is synonymous with nicotine dependency. Conclusively, dependency always involves abuse, but abuse does not necessarily imply dependency.

What is dependency?

Dependency is when an individual uses a substance regularly, and then, for one reason or another, does not have the means to use the desired substance, which results in physiological or psychological withdrawal symptoms that result from the inability to use. There are two types of dependency: psychological and physiological; and they are interactive. *Psychological dependency* is when an individual engages in certain behaviors, which occur regularly and then for one reason or another, the individual can no longer use the desired substance; the habitual user then experiences symptoms of psychological withdrawal (anxiety, depression, irritability, inability to concentrate, etc) that result from the absence of use.

The other type of dependency is physiological dependency. *Physiological dependency* is a state where the individual ingests a substance regularly, and the body becomes accustomed to the substance being present in the person's body. Further, other physiological functioning changes because of the presence of the ingested substance. When the substance is no longer present in the system, physiological dysfunction occurs, and the individual experiences withdrawal symptoms such as increased heart rate, sweating, tremors, diarrhea, and nausea. In my opinion, pornography addiction does not necessarily represent a physiological dependency because no foreign substances are being entered into the person's system. (I do not think it matters much in the context of its exploitative nature and its ability to hook susceptible individuals.) That is, compulsive pornography use represents a psychological dependency. A person compulsively viewing pornography is psychologically dependent upon its use.

Dependency is the state of needing a substance or person or behavior to function; this need is self-created by the individual that gets hooked. If your child is dependent on pornography use, then your child demonstrates certain symptoms, which will be discussed later in this chapter.

Dependency and addiction are related, but they are not necessarily the same thing. Dependency is always present in addiction, but addiction is not necessarily present in dependency. Meaning that some individuals can be dependent on certain substances or a certain person in their life and still live functional lives in modern-day society. For example, people can drink coffee or vaporize plant material and still experience success in the real world. These individuals are dependent upon caffeine or another plant material; yet still can function and some do very well in modern-day society. Do these people have an addiction? Not by the true definition. The definition of an *addiction* is habitually engaging in risky behaviors despite the negative consequences; when those consequences negatively impact many aspects of the individual's life, the social, psychological, and physiological, the person has an addiction. Addiction is a biopsychosocial phenomenon where compulsive use leads to the deterioration of many aspects of the individual's life.

In biology, dependence refers to the physiological adaptation to the presence of a substance in the organism's system. Ultimately, dependency boils down to withdrawal symptoms. If the individual has withdrawal symptoms from not having the substance or not engaging in the behavior, they have a dependency on that substance or behavior. If a person experiences an absence of use and experiences withdrawal symptoms, then the individual is dependent upon its use or dependent upon that behavior.

What is a compulsion?

Compulsions are behaviors that are repeated with seemingly no rational motivation, but these behaviors are performed in an attempt to reduce anxiety or soothe an obsession. Addiction involves the inability to stop the behavior, despite the negative consequences associated with the individual's use. Both compulsions and addictions involve a lack of impulse control.

A compulsion is a behavior that is designed to reduce stress or discomfort due to mental health symptoms such as depression or anxiety. Individuals engaging in compulsive behavior feel an irresistible need to engage in the behavior. For example, everyday behaviors such as hand-washing, cleaning, and counting can become compulsions.

Compulsive behaviors are actions that are engaged in repetitively, even when the person wishes that they could stop. Even though the compulsive behaviors result in negative consequences, lead to interpersonal conflicts, and even harm the individual's state of well-being, the individual continues to engage in the behavior because their mind is preoccupied with the substance or behavior. Common activities that can develop into compulsions include shopping, ordering, eating, gambling, sex, pornography, and exercise. Some of these behaviors are easier to overindulge in than others and some people get hooked on the aforementioned behaviors to the point where the social, psychological, and physiological aspects of their lives deteriorate. A well-known example of engaging in obsessive-compulsive behavior is a person who repeatedly checks the stove and oven range to ensure that it is turned off or constantly checking the door to ensure that it is locked. Engaging in compulsive behaviors rarely decreases anxiety in the long term. More times than not, engagement in compulsive behavior only provides temporary relief, but this relief is an illusion, and it passes quickly. In some cases, compulsive behavior starts to consume a person's entire life.

What is addiction?

Addiction is a biological, social, and physiological phenomenon where the individual experiences major dysfunction in one or more areas of their life because of their compulsive use. Addiction is a challenging situation for the individual and generally requires a lifelong effort to overcome it and achieve and maintain sobriety.

Addiction is a progressive condition, a disease of the brain. Addiction manifests itself through compulsive use of a substance or process behavior, regardless of the harmful consequences experienced by its users. A person with a *process addiction* (or a *behavioral addiction*) is hooked on a certain process or behavior that yields predictable results. Process addictions include dependency on gambling, shopping/spending money, sex, internet pornography, gaming, and food. Further, people struggling with addiction obsessively focus on using, to the point that their addiction completely controls nearly every aspect of their life. The addicted individual continues to use despite the problems that are created in their life. Even though there needs to be further research into treatments for pornography use dysfunction, effective modalities for recovery from pornography addiction are available, and people do recover from their problematic use of pornography. The book is designed to move your child and you towards recovery.

People compulsively using often display distorted thinking, abnormal behaviors, and dysfunctional ways of relating to other people. Changes in the brain's wiring cause people to have intense urges to use and make it challenging for the individual to stop their use. Brain imaging studies show long-term changes in the areas of the brain for chronic users that are responsible for judgment, decision-making, learning, memory, and impulse control.[27] Adolescents begin to use pornography for several reasons, including to feel good, to feel better, to escape their reality, out of curiosity, and peer pressure.

---

[27] Volkow, N. D., Fowler, J. S., & Wang, G. J. (2003). The addicted human brain: insights from imaging studies. *The Journal of clinical investigation, 111*(10), 1444-1451.

Symptomology and Pornography Addiction

Pornography addiction is considered a conduct, behavioral, or process addiction where the dependent individual has urges and impulses to use pornographic content - to the point where they have problems in their life that result from its use.

Question: "What is pornography addiction referred to as?"

Response: Pornography Use Disorder does not appear in the *Diagnostic Statistical Manual of Mental Disorders* (DSM), which is published by the American Psychiatric Association; the DSM is a scientific classification guide for mental health disorders. As a clinician in the field of chemical dependency, I already see patients who compulsively use pornography, the internet, and their smartphone. They report to me that their chronic consumption of internet pornography is harmful to their life. The only behavioral addiction that appears in the DSM-5 is a gambling disorder (gambling addiction, problematic gambling). The following criteria serve as my prediction about what is going to be included in an upcoming edition of the DSM for its diagnosis of Pornography Use Disorder.

My prediction of symptoms is based upon my study and treatment of Substance Use Disorder, coupled with my knowledge of symptoms related to obsessions and compulsions. I am well versed in addiction, particularly pornography addiction. Psychiatrists, mental health therapists, and scientists are looking at the research now to figure out what symptoms to include in a future edition of the DSM as part of its diagnosis of Pornography Use

Disorder. The harmful effects of compulsive pornography use have been shown in the literature time and time again. There are many harms associated with the consumption of internet pornography and that is explained in a later part of the text. Symptoms of problematic pornography use (or Pornography Use Disorder) include:

- Inability to reduce or stop use (loss of control, unmanageability)
    - Does your child have a history of attempting to reduce or stop use and has been unsuccessful?
    - Has your child tried to stop in the past and was unsuccessful?
    - Is your child unable to significantly reduce or stop their use?
- Causes harm to relationships
    - Has your child's use negatively impacted their self-esteem?
    - If your child has a Significant Other, does the SO object to their habitual use?
    - Has a sober friend complained to your child that they are not spending enough time with other people because of their use?
    - Are there relationships in your child's life that have been negatively impacted by their compulsive use?

- Failure to meet work, school, or home responsibilities
    - Is your child tired at school because of their chronic use? Is your child late to school because of their use?
    - Is your child unprepared for their academic exams because the time that was to be allocated for studying was spent using?
    - Have the grades of your child significantly dropped because of excessive pornography use?
    - Does your child not have enough time to clean their room because they are preoccupied with pornography?
    - Has your child been written up at school or work for a reason that relates to their chronic use?
- Withdrawal symptoms
    - If your child stops using pornography, do they have ill effects that result from an absence of use?
    - If your child is unable to compulsively use, do they experience irritability, anxiety, or depression?
- Tolerance to pornography use
    - Does your child view more pornography to achieve their desired effect?

- Does your child use the same amount of pornography over time and in time it produces less than their desired effect?
- Does your child use more extreme and violent forms of hardcore pornography to achieve their desired effect?

- A significant amount of time is spent on using pornography
  - Does your child spend a significant amount of time using pornography?
  - Is your child giving up hobbies that they once enjoyed to use?

- Leads to or exacerbates underlying psychological or physiological problems
  - Has your child's sexual functioning been harmed by their use of pornography?
  - Does your child use pornography to escape uncomfortable emotions?
  - Does your child attempt to cover up their emotions by using pornography?
  - Has your child's mental health symptoms worsened because of their use?
  - If your adolescent feels rejected, do they then go use?

- Compulsions to use (compulsivity)
  - Does your child feel urges or cravings to use internet pornography?

- Does your child regularly get triggered to use?
- Justification and rationalization of your child's use (irrational thinking, cognitive distortions)
    - "I habitually use pornography because the potential sexual partners I meet are freezers."
    - "If I could get laid, I wouldn't have to use as much pornography."
    - "My pornography habit is okay because I only use porn that is female-friendly."
    - "It is okay to use because the women performers have smiles on their faces when they are being physically and psychologically abused."
    - "It is okay to view pornography objectifying and commodifying women because the performers are paid."
    - "I am allowed to use pornography because my ex 'did me wrong'."
    - "I work hard, so I am allowed to relax by watching at least one porn scene each day."
    - "My buddy spends 4 hours a day consuming porn and I only use it for 2 hours a day. He might have a problem; but I do not have a problem."
- Used pornography dangerously

- Has your child dangerously used pornography?
  - While driving a car?
  - While cutting off airflow to the brain? (Autoerotic asphyxiophilia)
  - While at work or at school?
- Continued use despite experiencing negative consequences
  - Does your child continue to chronically use pornography, despite having problems with relationships, time management, finances, motivation, etc.?

If your child meets two or three of the criteria, then your child has a mild form of pornography use dysfunction. Four to five of the criteria, their disorder is considered moderate; if your child meets the criteria for six or more, then your child exhibits a severe form of pornography addiction. Even if your child exhibits symptoms indicating a severe form of pornography addiction, this book contains knowledge that can help liberate your child from the bondage imposed by high-speed internet pornography; your child's recovery is doable if they can work for it, one day at a time. One day at a time is key. Conclusively, pornography addiction is the state where a person compulsively uses pornography, and their use is detrimental to their psychological, social, and physiological wellbeing; pornography addiction is when a person habitually uses pornography and loses interest in other activities because of their preoccupation with consuming pornography.

Why is Internet Pornography Addictive?

High-speed internet pornography is like a drug; the use of pornography is similar to that of cocaine. When a person uses pornography, the onset of the rush is rapid. The feeling of the high is intense. The high is short-lived. The dopamine is released, it rushes through the brain, and then it washes out relatively quickly. Research analyzing the neuroimaging data of participants who viewed internet pornography showed brain region activation similar to craving and drug cue reactions for alcohol, cocaine, and nicotine. Viewing pornography, especially when it is done compulsively, activates the same neural networks as for alcohol and other drugs.[28]

Not everyone who drinks alcohol becomes addicted. The same can also be said for internet pornography. Not everyone who views pornography will use pornography compulsively. As reviewed in the next chapter, viewing pornography portraying sexual objectification and commodification of women is not a victimless act.

The consumption of high-speed internet pornography is very powerful because when a person uses pornography, the brain releases a chemical known as dopamine. *Dopamine* is a chemical released in the brain that makes the person feel pleasure and motivates the individual to actively approach life. At that point, viewing pornography (which is usually coupled with solo masturbation and ejaculation for its users) acts like a drug in the brain; using pornography can be very rewarding for

---

[28] Love, T., Laier, C., Brand, M., Hatch, L., & Hajela, R. (2015). Neuroscience of Internet pornography addiction: A review and update. *Behavioral sciences*, 5(3), 388-433.

some groups of people. In research exploring the neuroscience of pornography use, the researchers found that participants in the study who viewed internet pornography showed activation in the brain similar to the craving and drug cue reactions as with alcohol, cocaine, and nicotine. The pornography acted in the same way as these drugs. That is, individuals can become psychologically dependent on internet pornography because sex and pornography use provide a reward (large release of dopamine) to the user and the reward motivates the user to continue the behavior, despite its unproductive nature.

Some people can responsibly use alcohol and they never develop abuse, dependency, or addiction. They are in control over their alcohol use and nothing ever comes of it; they have put alcohol in its place. The same might be true for pornography, but then some people get hooked on it. Some people tending to have compulsions and obsessions are susceptible to forming a dependency on internet pornography. Pornography is addictive because it reinforces the individual to continue using it; pornography use reinforces itself. There is a pay-off associated with using pornography. The brain releases a surge of dopamine, and the individual feels a sort of high from it. The act of viewing pornography, which is often coupled with solo masturbation and ejaculation, is rewarding to the primitive brain; yet, it is not in the person's best interest to receive this kind of reward for doing nothing. Doing this demotivates the individual regarding the achievement of meaningful goals.

When a person is dependent upon their consumption of internet pornography, the brain is depleted of dopamine, serotonin, and norepinephrine. In turn, when the individual is engaging in mundane things in life or having mildly pleasant experiences, these experiences become dull and colored by gray because of the lack of dopamine and other feel-good chemicals in the brain. In chronic users, those feel-good chemicals are not released naturally because they have been artificially released by their pornography use.

As with other forms of addiction, when people compulsively use pornography, they release dopamine, serotonin, and norepinephrine; when an individual regularly watches pornography and ejaculates, the user squanders their vital life energy and becomes weak. A person who chronically ejaculates to pornography loses the ability to be strong and full of energy. When a person frees themselves from compulsive masturbation and pornography use, they have the opportunity to become strong and resilient again; when the individual honors their vital life energy, they are setting themselves up for success.

Being addicted to pornography is bondage; it is mental slavery. When I was addicted to pornography, I was a servant to my out of control mind. My mind had control of me; I had not yet mastered my mind. The regular consumption of internet pornography affects many aspects of the user's life and can make them feel powerless. The addiction becomes unmanageable. As a parent or caregiver, encourage your child to triumph over their pornography addiction. Your child will learn to overcome their compulsive use of masturbation and pornography through regular motivation, honesty with themselves and others, and compassionate and non-judgmental accountability. Through living out these ways from here on out, your child will recover from their pornography addiction. You are a part of your child's in-person social support system; meaning, you are in a great position to matter-of-factly hold them accountable. You can be there for your child so that they can free themselves from the mental chains, and you can help your child experience liberation from addiction once again.

Dependency on internet pornography

If your child has come to you because they think that they have a problem with their pornography use, you should feel very thankful that your child has come to you wanting help. At this point, your child is already in a really good position to recover from their compulsive use of pornography. You can be a part of your child's support system that helps hold them accountable in a compassionate way, so they have the tools that they need to recover. This book has been published for you to have the background, the terminology, and the knowledge needed to support your child in overcoming their compulsive use. If you are a parent and you have evidence to indicate that your child regularly visits pornography websites and they are hiding their behavior, this is more of a challenging situation; with the proper approach and follow-through, anything is possible. You can support your child and present them with tools that they need to overcome addiction.

As mentioned earlier in this chapter, psychological dependency on pornography use is classified as a process addiction. Further, addiction involves repetitiveness, high frequency, and excessive use, whether focusing on a substance or behavior. Some of the signs of process addictions mimic those of a substance use disorder. Those include:

- Tolerance
- Withdrawal symptoms
- Inability to stop use
- Use is the primary focus of the individual's life
- Behavioral addiction

If your child wants to recover, then they have to be open and teachable; they need to be able to listen. For your child to hear you, you have to approach them with a desire to understand their experience. Finding out why your child is doing what they are doing is critical to helping your child. Your child might not even know why they do what they are doing. Finding out why the behavior is taking place will allow your child to go back to the root of the issue; a trained therapist or psychologist is the best route to go for identifying the root of the compulsive use.

There is some underlying mechanism that needs to be resolved for the addiction to be healed. So getting individual therapy from a mental health therapist is something that you should consider for your child. This is a guide designed to help you raise awareness about your child's problematic pornography use and gear them towards treatment if they are interested. Even though people can overcome their behavioral addiction through support groups, a positive social network, and non-judgmental accountability, individual therapy is something that cannot be replaced. Social connection cannot replace therapy, and therapy cannot replace social connections. In conclusion, therapy, support groups, and compassionate accountability are key ingredients in recovery.

This is a guidebook that will give you the language and the skills to reinforce positive behaviors and shape behaviors in such a way that incentivizes sobriety. This text explains reinforcement and how you can apply free and low-cost incentives to your child when they are making progress in recovery. This is where accountability comes into play. You can monitor your child's internet use by using accountability software to monitor which sites they visit. This level of accountability will allow your child to feel safe within the boundaries you set, and then they make personal choices. This gives your child the free will to make choices and it allows them to think about the consequences associated with their behaviors.

You can shape behaviors that will increase the likelihood your child experiences success in the social, psychological, and physiological domains of their life. You can help your child to triumph over their pornography addiction through unconditional positive regard. This may mean that you need to do some work on yourself before you can take an active role in assisting your child in their recovery from compulsive pornography use. This means introspection, looking inside of yourself to see what you need to resolve, so you can put yourself in the best position to gently approach your child's addiction. Being kind, compassionate, and non-judgmental might be second nature to you, and that is great. Teachable parents can learn the skills that are needed to compassionately intervene in this sort of situation. This book and guide give you the skills to be able to assist your child in reducing and hopefully eliminating their habitual use of internet pornography.

Harms Associated with Internet Pornography Use

"The psychological effects that pornography has on the mind cannot be denied; the harm done to both the viewer and the viewed cannot be denied. It is critical to address today's pornographic culture for what it is: a hub for sex-trafficking and a gateway drug for future pimps and johns."[29] ~Katie Tomkiewicz, a women's advocate, blogger

Resulting from addiction, much dysfunction occurs in the user's and the family's life. Addiction affects most, if not all areas of an individual's life: the psychological, the social, and the physiological. When a person is addicted, they tend to be unable to hold stable relationships with other people. If your child is addicted to pornography, then it may be very challenging for them to establish and maintain a healthy relationship with another person, especially in the context of a mature, romantic relationship.

Being addicted to pornography significantly decreases the likelihood that the addicted individual can be emotionally available to their partner. Being addicted to pornography negatively affects a person's decision making. For example, your child may be out and about, and then have an opportunity to strike up a conversation

---

[29] Tomkiewicz, K. (2016, July 27). Pornography and Sex-Trafficking: One and the Same. Retrieved August 29, 2020, from
https://www.redeeminglovecа.com/new-blog/2016/7/24/pornography-and-sex-trafficking-one-and-the-same

with a young person of their sexual preference, then decides not to approach the potential partner because they are thinking in the back of their mind, "I don't need to take the risk of interacting with this real person because I can always view pornography to get my rocks off. Porn is safe." In this situation, your child is choosing pornography over an interaction with a real-life individual. I know this thought takes place because it happened to me more than once. After witnessing this happen to me multiple times and now being aware of my thoughts, I knew I needed to make a change. When a person is making those kinds of choices, the odds of living a worthwhile life are no longer in the individual's favor. That's how the Universe works.

Dysfunction created through pornography addiction

Regular use of internet pornography is linked to sexual violence. Studies have shown that people who view pornography tend to support statements that promote abuse and violence toward women and girls.[30] Multiple studies have shown that exposure to both violent and nonviolent pornography increases aggressive behavior, including both having violent fantasies and committing violent offenses.[31] "Exposure to pornography, in general, has been linked with adolescent dating violence and

---

[30] Hald, G. M., Malamuth, N. M., & Yuen, C. (2010). Pornography and attitudes supporting violence against women: Revisiting the relationship in nonexperimental studies. Aggressive Behavior: Official Journal of the International Society for Research on Aggression, 36(1), 14-20.

[31] Wright, P. J., Tokunaga, R. S., & Kraus, A. (2016). A meta-analysis of pornography consumption and actual acts of sexual aggression in general population studies. *Journal of Communication*, *66*(1), 183-205.

sexual aggression."[32] There is more research that shows pornography exposure and its link to sexual violence. The internet sites, FightTheNewDrug.com and TruthAboutPorn.org are great resources for tracking down the scientific literature that provides empirical data linking pornography use and violence.

Other harms associated with the regular use of internet pornography include decreased exposure to interactions with other people. That is, choosing masturbation and pornography sessions over interactions with potential sexual partners and mates is a major obstacle for your child's development. Your addicted love one is opting out of an in-person interaction and relationship with a real person for a bastardized version of a sexual experience. For its users, chronic use of pornography is often paired with masturbation and ejaculation. Frequent ejaculation, especially via manual release (masturbation), needlessly wastes the person's vital life energy; it significantly reduces the mastorbators ability to manifest a rich and full life. In other words, regularly viewing pornography while masturbating and ejaculating and living a prosperous life do relate to one another; that is, a person cannot have it both ways. It is a choice between pornography or love.

If you intend to raise a child who experiences success as an adult, address your child's use of internet pornography. Some specific harms stemming from pornography use and solo masturbation include:

---

[32] Rostad, W. L., Gittins-Stone, D., Huntington, C., Rizzo, C. J., Pearlman, D., & Orchowski, L. (2019). The association between exposure to violent pornography and teen dating violence in grade 10 high school students. *Archives of sexual behavior*, *48*(7), 2137-2147.

- Lethargy, depression, anxiety, loneliness, and other mental health symptoms[33] [34]
- Decreased ability to relate with people
- Decreased ability to maintain healthy relationships with loved ones and friends
- Increased likelihood of developing erectile or other sexual dysfunction
- Inability to serve as a potent individual in the world today
- Increased likelihood to support sexual aggression
- Inability to live one's highest good

To have these symptoms clear up for your child, follow the suggestions spelled out in this guide. In conclusion, habitual use of internet pornography is harmful to the individual user, women performers, and society at large.

Content produced by the pornography industry portrays the objectification, commodification, misogyny, degradation, and powerlessness of women. In an upcoming chapter, I will further flesh out the pornography industry's exploitation and debasement of women; pornography is harmful to the viewer, the viewed, and the family members because of the industry's exploitation of women. As distinguished linguist, philosopher, cognitive

---

[33] Yoder, V. C., VIRDEN III, T. B., & Amin, K. (2005). Internet pornography and loneliness: An association?. Sexual addiction & compulsivity, 12(1), 19-44.

[34] Butler, M. H., Pereyra, S. A., Draper, T. W., Leonhardt, N. D., & Skinner, K. B. (2018). Pornography use and loneliness: A bidirectional recursive model and pilot investigation. Journal of sex & marital therapy, 44(2), 127-137.

scientist, social critic, and political activist Noam Chomsky states, "As for the fact that [pornography]'s some people's erotica, well you know that's their problem... If they get enjoyment out of humiliation of women, they have a problem." If your child uses internet pornography, this guide is created for you; it will help you address and ideally remedy the situation. I have published this book because my heart goes out to you.

Readiness and Resistance to Change

As the parent, your child may pose resistance to you when you are talking to them about exposure to pornography. This is natural. Often, people struggling with addiction resist when the external environment is addressing their addiction. If your child resists recovery for their dysfunction, offer them more education about the topic. The more educated your child is about the harms associated with the use of internet pornography, the easier it will be for them to let go of their resistance to recovery. Denial is an integral part of the addiction process and cycle. As your child's parent, do not take this personally. Denial serves as a defense mechanism for your addicted loved one. Keep in mind that the sooner your child can rise above the misery of addiction, the better it will be for you both.

Most adolescents and people in general struggling with addiction have some resistance to the recovery process. This resistance or denial prevents them from reaching out for help. In many cases, this resistance to change will lead to a complete deterioration of their life; it sends them on a hopeless, self-destructive path. A path that leads to nowhere. If you are emotionally prepared to address your child's addiction to internet pornography, talk to your child. Your way of approaching the situation is probably going to look a little bit different than the next family's; but there are common elements that need to be present when addressing your child's compulsive use of internet pornography. If a parent is paying for their child's housing, it is my opinion that it is the parents' responsibility to compassionately address any addiction that their child may have. The parent is not forcing their child to recover; but the parent is significantly increasing the likelihood that their child will learn to use the internet in constructive ways.

The person struggling with addiction is the only person who can solve their issue. At the same time, community and a strong support network (whatever it looks like for your child) are needed to recover from their addiction. Over time, a person struggling with addiction will be able to see the harm that their addiction has caused in their lives, yet they still refuse to get help.

Self-efficacy is the degree to which the individual believes in their ability to achieve something meaningful. If your child's self-efficacy is low, this means your child does not believe it is possible to achieve meaningful goals. This lack of confidence in your child's self-perception of their ability to recover will cause them to remain resistant to the idea of giving up pornography. As a parent and the most highly influential person in your child's life, you can increase the likelihood that your child will experience an increase in self-efficacy by acknowledging their interest and intention to achieve recovery. Observing their peers achieve the same goal of recovery in the context of a Twelve Steps fellowship or similar support group can also help your child increase their perceptions of self-efficacy.

Many times, people struggling with addiction justify their compulsive use of the substance or the process behavior. Common roots of resistance include denial that their habitual use creates significant harm in their life. People struggling with addiction justify their use of internet pornography because they are misusing the behavior to ineffectively cope with their problems in life. Your child sees themself as responding to the suffering they are experiencing and does not see that their chronic use of pornography is contributing to the suffering they experience. If your adolescent has lost a romantic relationship with another young person, there is a tendency for your child to justify the use of their pornography as a means of dealing with the loss of a romantic relationship.

Often, people struggling with addiction see their compulsive use as their savior, instead of seeing it as one of the causes of their suffering. For some people struggling with addiction, they develop the irrational thought that their life is not bad because they know someone who does the same thing and their life is so much worse. When you detect that your child is visiting pornography sites, address the situation as early as possible. Further, compulsive use of pornography could develop into a much more severe form of sex addiction. Not addressing the situation would allow your child to continue with the escalating behavior and allow them to hit rock bottom as they have never experienced before. In the treatment of substance abuse, clinicians work to raise their client's rock bottom by using techniques such as motivational interviewing and motivational enhancement therapy.

In the Twelve Steps tradition, *rock bottom* is the lowest possible level; it is a horrible place where individuals struggling with addiction feel lost and confused. Rock bottom is a place where their entire life is in shambles. A state of being where addicted individuals feel as if they cannot sink any lower emotionally, psychologically, or physically. Rock bottom is the absolute lowest point one can reach in life. Rock bottom represents a state of absolute misery and wretchedness. Each person's rock bottom is different. This book is designed to raise the rock bottom of your child.

In motivational interviewing, motivational enhancement therapy, and other similar modalities, therapists get their clients to identify core values. Then, the clinician and client compare the core values to their behaviors and see if there is alignment between them or not. When the patient's behavior is different from what is reflected in their core values, clinicians use this gap to get the client to find the motivation they need to change their behavior. By showing your child the harm they have already endured through regular use of internet pornography, you can raise your child's rock bottom and motivate and inspire them to get help and initiate the recovery process.

Another reason people struggling with addiction have resistance to recovery is that they fear the unknown of recovery. They are miserable in their life, but there is comfort in the familiarity of it. People struggling with dependency issues know deep in their hearts that overcoming addiction involves major changes in their life and these types of major changes scare them. Also, people struggling with addiction tend to fear that sober life is boring. Your child may find it impossible to imagine how they can have fun and be happy without using internet pornography. Hopefully, your child realizes that the use of internet pornography is preventing them from naturally experiencing pleasure and contentment. Your child may fail to realize that regular pornography use is not making them happy. It is detracting from their peace of mind; viewing pornography is causing them to have a fiery mind. A mind that is never content, never satisfied. Additionally, your child may have already tried to get clean from their compulsive internet pornography use. Perhaps, your child has not been successful in their attempt to recover. Your child may not realize that because they were not successful with their first attempt in recovery, this does not mean that they cannot be successful this time around. Another reason your child may be trapped in their addiction is that they do not understand what recovery is all about. Your child may believe that recovery requires finding God or becoming a self-righteous health nut. Your child may fail to realize that there are many paths to recovery, and some of those paths will suit their needs and preferences.

More neurological research is needed into both the nature of pornography addiction and scientifically validated therapeutic modalities that are intended to treat mental health symptoms associated with its problematic use.

In this chapter, you learned:

Recovery and Authoritative Parenting

- Dependency is a state where the body or mind habituates to the presence of a substance or behavior that releases large amounts of dopamine, and when the person goes without, they experience withdrawal symptoms.

- Addiction is a bio-psycho-social phenomenon (often referred to as a brain disease) where the use of the drug or behavior creates significant harm in many aspects of the individual's life and the individual continues to use the substance or behavior despite the negative consequences associated with it.

- Symptoms of problematic pornography use include psychological dependency, tolerance, withdrawal symptoms, anhedonia, unmanageability, escapism, compulsions, and other mental health symptoms.

- Internet pornography is addictive to a significant portion of people using it because sex is rewarding; "free," online pornography can be found anywhere on the world wide web on any modern electronic device that does not utilize an installed filter.

- Dependency on internet pornography is described as a process addiction, meaning that the individual engages in a behavior or pattern of behaviors to elicit the dopamine rush (high) that they are seeking.

- Harms of pornography dependency include problems with loved ones, employment, finances, self-esteem, and self-efficacy.
- Addressing your child's dependency is a sensitive topic, and when doing so, handle the situation compassionately and non-judgmentally.
- By convincing themselves that their addiction does not cause problems in their life, people struggling with habitual use rationalize and justify their addictive behaviors.
- Monitoring your child's internet activity allows you to hold them accountable for their behaviors.

Chapter 3
Recovery and Authoritative Parenting

What is Recovery?

Recovery is the process in which an individual significantly reduces and hopefully eliminates the use of the drug or addictive behaviors and also significantly improves the psychological, physiological, and social aspects of their life. Recovery includes significantly reducing and hopefully eliminating use of a substance or process behavior. Further, recovery is also a practice or way of life that transcends the prevention of destructive use of substances or in this case, internet pornography. Recovery involves changing both old thought patterns and behaviors that contributed to and fueled the individual's addiction. In *Alcoholics Anonymous*, the largest and original Twelve Steps program, there is a term called a *dry drunk*. In the recovery movement, a *dry drunk* is an individual who abstains from drinking or using, yet does not change any of their thoughts or behaviors that brought and kept them in addiction. Recovery is a journey that is embarked upon by the struggling individual.

Recovery is going beyond what the dry drunk does to abstain from drinking. Ideally, recovery involves healing the trauma that the individual may have experienced. Recovering from addiction consists of making amends with people that have been hurt by the individual's addiction. The process of recovery involves finding out what the individual's core values and passions are in life. To move forward in recovery, the person has to figure out what lights them up on the inside. Recovery touches upon all aspects of an individual's life; it involves healing the mind, body, and spirit.

In the professional treatment world, recovery is a step forward as compared to the old idea of rehabilitation. The *rehabilitation* model views addicted individuals as broken and their treatment will rehabilitate them and fix their brokenness. Recovery is a much more holistic approach. The model of recovery recognizes addiction as a brain disease and must be addressed on the medical, psychiatric, societal, familial, and psychological levels. When treating addiction, the patient's treatment care team needs to practice compassion and non-judgment so the individual can address what they need to in life to recover. In summary, recovery from addiction is:

- gradual;
- taking things day by day;
- taking action in the Stages of Change;
- addressing unresolved trauma;
- being honest with oneself and other people;
- being reliable and dependable;
- experiencing contentment and joy without relying on substance use or behavioral addictions;
- living a life that contributes to the wellbeing of society, family, friends, and oneself;
- about giving back to groups of people that need assistance;
- striving to have alignment with one's thoughts, words, and actions.

Conclusively, recovery is a personal journey rather than a destination that involves developing: hope, a secure base and sense of self, supportive relationships, empowerment, social inclusion, coping skills, and meaning.[35]

Connection is the remedy

There is no quick fix for addiction; if there was, it would have been found already. There is no cure-all for a person who is dependent on a substance or behavioral addiction. Recovery from addiction can only be achieved by significantly reducing or eliminating use.

To fully recover from addiction, addicted individuals need to process any unresolved trauma. If your child has any trauma or suffering that they need to process, the care of a licensed mental health therapist in your state is appropriate. Contact your insurance company or visit PsychologyToday.com to search for licensed counselors, therapists, and psychologists.

When speaking of recovery, I, of course, have to mention Twelve Steps approach to recovery. A Twelve Step program is a set of guiding principles and actions involving connection and accountability; the purpose of the group is to support people in overcoming addiction, compulsion, or other problematic behavior. Generally, a Twelve Step program is an abstinence-based accountability system. Alcoholics Anonymous (AA) originally proposed the twelve-step fellowship as a

---

[35] Elm, J. H., Lewis, J. P., Walters, K. L., & Self, J. M. (2016). "I'm in this world for a reason": Resilience and recovery among American Indian and Alaska Native two-spirit women. Journal of lesbian studies, 20(3-4), 352-371.

method of abstaining from alcohol use and recovering from its destructive effects. The American Psychological Association summarizes the Twelve Steps as follows:

- Admit that the individual cannot control their addictive use
- Recognize that a higher power can give the individual strength over their addiction
- Examine past errors with the assistance of a sponsor, experienced member
- Make amends and apologize for the errors made during addiction
- Learn to live a new life with an ethical code of conduct
- Give back and help others who suffer from the same addiction[36]

In conclusion, a Twelve Step program serves as guidelines highlighting a path for recovery from addiction, compulsion, or other behavioral problems.

A person struggling with dependency issues attends a few meetings and then starts to like the meetings because they see familiar faces greeting them. The individual feels good about going to the meetings, and in turn, this reinforces their abstinence. The recovering individual enjoys and feels good about attending the meetings. It is easier for the recoveree to adhere to abstinence; thus, they in turn, go to the meetings and feel even better because their fellow members congratulate them on staying clean.

---

[36] VandenBos, G. R. (2007). *APA dictionary of psychology*. American Psychological Association.

They feel connected with the people in their fellowship. The perceived hole that the person was trying to fill with drugs, alcohol, pornography, etc., is now filled with intentional meetings and meaningful interactions with people they relate with. The recoveree forms fellowship with individuals in the group and looks forward to the meetings. Examples of Twelve Step fellowships that focus on sex and pornography addiction are listed:

- Sex and Love Addicts Anonymous (SLAA)
- Sex Addicts Anonymous (SAA)
- Sexaholics Anonymous (SA)
- Porn Addicts Anonymous (PAA)

Perform a Google search of these Twelve Step Fellowship organizations to see if they have a local chapter in your area. PAA is strictly an online fellowship, so anyone from anywhere can have support. Also, that is one of the beautiful things about NoFap; anyone in the world can access its resources. (NoFap.com is a website and online community forum that serves as a support group for individuals who are interested in avoiding the use of pornography and masturbation). Additional resources about online AA meetings can be obtained via the Intergroup website of Alcoholics Anonymous. This website contains a list and corresponding links to online AA meetings that are happening at all hours of the night and day. Visit https://aa-intergroup.org/oiaa/meetings/ for more information about online meetings for AA.

Question from a parent: "Isn't AA for people struggling with alcohol abuse? Why would my child, who does not drink, attend an online AA meeting?"

Response: Yes, Alcoholics Anonymous is a fellowship for people struggling with alcohol problems, yet, I have known many of my patients who are in recovery from opioid dependency who attend AA meetings. People struggling with addiction from drugs or other behaviors attend AA meetings because there are more AA meetings than compared to any other fellowship. Further, addiction is an addiction. It does not matter if the person is dependent upon alcohol, fentanyl, gambling, or pornography, the person who compulsively uses a substance is doing so in an attempt to escape their current reality. Further, escapist behaviors lead to nowhere. If a person is drinking or using to escape their current version of reality, then participation in a Twelve Step Fellowship or similar support group is helpful. In-person meetings are so much better, but, an online meeting is way better than no meeting at all.

Alcoholics Anonymous was the first Twelve Step Fellowship and is the largest and most widespread support group in the world. On a side note, when I participate in an online AA meeting, I change the word from "drink" to "use." The fellow members are always happy when I participate and share. As stated previously, to recover, an individual needs honesty, accountability, and motivation to change. When a person struggling with an addiction participates in a Twelve Step fellowship, those conditions are met and the individual has what it takes to recover.

Authoritative Parenting

Authoritative parenting is a style of parenting characterized by being highly responsive to your child and having high expectations of your child's behavior.

Authoritative parents take responsibility for their child's emotional needs while having certain standards governing their child's behavior. Authoritative parents set clear limitations and boundaries for their child's behavior and they are consistent in enforcing boundaries. Authoritative parents:

- are warm, in tune with the emotional needs of their child, and are nurturing;
- listen to their child;
- allow and encourage independence and autonomy;
- reason with their child instead of making their child blindly obey;
- set clear limits and boundaries on their child's behavior;
- consistently enforce the rules;
- use positive discipline instead of punitive measures such as corporal punishment;
- do not put themselves in a position where they are demanding their child's respect;
- earn the trust and the respect of their child by giving them choices and opportunities to make errors and learn from them;
- communicate expectations regarding their child's behavior;
- realize that their child is not going to meet their expectations all of the time;
- raise well-rounded and socially-fit children.

When the child does not meet expectations, authoritative parents address the matter based on facts; there is no judgment involved. If you have not already, addressing your child's misbehaviors is a skill that you can learn.

Generally, authoritative parenting produces the best outcomes in children. Parents with an authoritative style tend to raise children who as adults tend to:

- to be content;
- be independent and self-reliant;
- have developed social skills;
- have positive ways for emotional regulation and self-control;
- express compassion and cooperation with others;
- explore new environments without fear;
- be competent and assertive.

Conclusively, authoritative parenting is an approach that combines warmth, sensitivity, and limit setting. Authoritative parents use discussion, reasoning, and positive reinforcement to guide children and avoid resorting to threats or punishments.

Have House Rules

Question from a parent: "Why is having house rules important?"

Response: House rules are positive statements about how the family decides to look after and treat its members. House rules help children and adolescents learn what behaviors are acceptable and what behaviors are not acceptable. To assist your child, be consistent in your discipline. Household rules can help everyone in the family get along better and they make family life more positive and more peaceful.

Question from a parent: "How do I implement house rules if our family has never had them before?"

Response: Have a sit-down discussion with your family. As you are your child's parent, you have to have the authority to initiate the formation and implementation of house rules. Explain how having house rules helps your family members learn what behaviors are desired and what behaviors are undesired. Explain that family rules help each family member get along with each other much more easily. House rules allow for more spaciousness and ease in family life. Having house rules sends the message that each member has a part to fulfill in family life. House rules help ensure that each family member's needs are met.

When putting together your family's house rules, get buy-in from your child. Ask your child what kinds of rules would be good rules. Listen to your child's response. Reflect on what your child said to you. Show your child that you are listening to them. When children (and adults as well) are heard and validated, they are much more likely to display acceptance and compliance to the agreed-upon house rules.

If your child is currently more influential than you are in your home and "calls the shots," take back your authority as the parent. Explain your role as a parent. Do it gently; explain the situation matter-of-factly. Avoid

Recovery and Authoritative Parenting

letting it devolve into a power struggle. Developing your relationship with your child, not allowing your frustration to show, being kind, explaining your reasoning, and giving your child options are ways to avoid power struggles with your child.

It seems that parents have a responsibility to have and implement house rules. In turn, parents have a responsibility to do their best to educate and guide their children toward constructive behaviors. By reading a book like this, you are taking responsibility for your circumstances and are willing to do what it takes to help your child. Mentoring and parenting the youth can be viewed as one of the most important jobs that we have in society.

Conscious humans have a responsibility to raise the youth with values that are conducive to human happiness and equality on Earth. Approaches, techniques, and tips reviewed in this book are needed for recovery from addiction. As stated, this guide is specifically created for adults with an adolescent loved one who is struggling with the problematic use of pornography.

If you do not have house rules, have a discussion about it and how they are important in raising a child who is successful in their personal and professional life. Here are some examples of house rules:

- Treat all people with dignity and respect.
- Before making plans outside the home, ask permission.
- Before borrowing something, ask permission.

- Before entering a bedroom, knock on the door and wait for a response.
- Be honest and truthful.
- Listen and do what you say you are going to do.
- Pitch in and do your chores.
- Before playing, complete your chores and homework.
- Take responsibility for your living space.
- Keep your body, mind, and living space clean.
- Pick up and clean up after yourself.
- Use the internet for constructive purposes.
- Follow the family car rules.
- If you are going to disagree, do it politely.
- When you make a mistake, you are responsible for fixing it.

Each one of these rules helps the child to be successful; family rules exist to help the child experience compassion, health, happiness, productivity, and success. Create similar rules or feel free to use these rules with your adolescent. With younger children, have around 5 simple rules. For adolescents, have up to 9 rules and those can be a little bit more in depth. Further, write the rules down. Display them in a common area where each family member can easily view the rules. If you need to, point to the rules; remind your child of them.

Talk about the positive benefits of having rules and how it teaches children to be more successful in their environment. Form the rules together with your child, listen and receive input from your son or daughter, and orient their perspective into the rules.

Question from a parent: "How do I detect that my child visits pornography sites? That is, I suspect that my child uses the internet to access pornography, but I am not sure. How can I find out if my child uses the internet to access pornography?"

Response: Build your relationship with your child. You need to have a foundation within the relationship so you are in the proper position to inform your child that you are going to start monitoring their internet use. When you have a solid foundation in your relationship with your child and you ask them to monitor their internet behavior and to set up an accountability program, your child will be much more likely to accept and adopt it. Your child will be much more likely to get behind the internet accountability program because you have this foundation on which you can build upon.

Then, in informal and formal discussions, start raising your child's awareness about the harms associated with using internet pornography. Create a conversation about the subject and educate your child. At this point, you are not directly asking them if they use internet pornography; you are simply creating a conversation around the topic of pornography, so your child becomes more aware. When your child and you are aware of both the nature of the pornography industry and the harms associated with the use of pornography portraying sexual objectification and commodification of women, your child can more easily modify their behavior and use the internet for constructive purposes.

Be transparent that you are going to monitor your child's use of the internet. Inform your child that you are going to monitor their internet behavior. Say "In one week or one month, your parents will be monitoring your internet behaviors. We are going to install certain apps to help keep you safe." Your child might be able to change their behaviors simply by knowing now that you are going to be monitoring their use of the internet. When your child knows that their internet activity is going to be monitored, and they persist by visiting pornography sites, this is an indicator that your child has a dependency on internet pornography or they simply do not care about adhering to the rules. As the parent, you have an authoritative role in the construction and implementation of the accountability program.

There are enough accountability software programs on the market that can help you teach your child to constructively use the internet. In a later chapter, the most widely-distributed software programs are listed. Next, implement the house rules. Explain that you pay for their housing, and it is part of your responsibility to do your best to set them up for success. To assist your child in overcoming their pornography addiction, you have to take back your parent-power as the authoritative leader in the relationship and in the long run, your child will respect and love you for it. As your child grows to the age of 18 to 25, your child will become an independent adult, and this is when you let go of your authoritative role in the relationship, and your spouse and you work on seeing your adult child as an autonomous individual. To have a relationship where you see your adult child as a completely sovereign person, they have to be financially, emotionally, and psychologically independent.

Question from a parent: "My child says that they only use 'female-friendly' porn and that kind of porn is not bad. How do I address this?"

Response: Even though 'female-friendly' pornography is marketed to be used by women and couples, the genre still depicts objectification and commodification of women. Most forms of modern pornography that are available on the world wide web portray the sexual objectification of men and women. Most female-friendly forms of commercial, mainstream pornography still end the scene with the *money shot*, i.e., the man ejaculating, likely on the face or breasts of the woman. The title of *female-friendly pornography* is terribly misleading. Objectifying a person continues the suffering of the one who is objectifying; also, it creates hostility amongst the objectifier and the objectified. Research shows that sexual objectification is harmful to people exposed to objectification. One study states that the "findings provided consistent evidence that both laboratory exposure and regular, everyday exposure to this content [portraying the objectification of women] are directly associated with a range of consequences, including higher levels of body dissatisfaction, greater self-objectification, greater support of sexist beliefs and of adversarial sexual beliefs, and greater tolerance of sexual violence toward women".[37] "Female-friendly"

---

[37] Ward, L. M. (2016). Media and sexualization: State of empirical research, 1995–2015. *The Journal of Sex Research*, *53*(4-5), 560-577.

pornography is a genre that glamorizes the objectification and commodification of women and thus, is a misnomer.

Before you use computer software to monitor your child's use of the internet, have a solid foundation with your son or daughter. If your child is young, I encourage you to put a filter on your child's account; yet, for adolescents aged 16 and older, I encourage monitoring, not censoring your child's internet behaviors. Through monitoring and holding your adolescent accountable for their behaviors, you are teaching your child how to be successful when you are not there. You are teaching your child how to be successful when they are not censored. Censorship does not teach anything. It sets up a scenario where your child could be inclined to "game the system" and work around the internet filters. For families, I encourage you to set up a separate account on the computer or laptop for each child; then, depending on your child's age, you can apply a specific filter or history tracking function for your child's internet activity. Consider only giving your child internet access through one device, whether it be through a tablet or a laptop. When discussing pornography, you can ask your child questions such as:

- When you are using the internet, have any pornography-related pop-ups appeared on the screen?
- Do any of your peers talk about looking at pornography?
- On purpose or accidentally, have you been exposed to pornography?

Recovery and Authoritative Parenting

- Do you think pornography portrays equality amongst men and women and all people in general?
- Do you think pornography sex is like how people really have sex?
- Do you know what objectification and commodification are?
- What questions do you have about pornography?
- What questions do you have?

Ask your child to think critically about the subject. Engage in a discussion about the nature of sex and pornography and talk about the harms associated with regular pornography use. Find articles online to discuss with your child. FightTheNewDrug.com is a great resource for parents and those who are addicted to pornography.

At this point, you are not directly asking your child if they use internet pornography, you are creating a conversation and discussion around the topics. Then, when you ask your child to monitor and to set up an accountability program with them, your child will be much more likely to adopt your motions toward internet accountability and transition into it more smoothly. Here are things that you do in order to address the situation:

1. Build your relationship with your child
    a. Spend quality time with them
2. Be able to talk about the harms associated with chronic pornography use

a. Study the material in this book
   b. Familiarize yourself with the content on sites such as FightTheNewDrug.com, NoFap.com, GailDines.com, and YourBrainOnPorn.com
3. Regularly discuss family values
   a. Explain why your family values what it does
4. Ask questions and create a conversation around the subject of pornography
   a. Listen and consider your child's input
5. Educate your child on the harms associated with the use of internet pornography
6. Discuss expectations, rules, consequences, and rewards
   a. Establish the house and internet rules
7. Monitor your child's internet activity
   a. Install the accountability software or router
      a. Which sites does your child regularly visit?
      b. Which search terms does your child insert into the search engine?
8. Provide accountability
   a. If your child visits pornography sites:
      a. Talk about what happened
      b. Optionally, remove privileges

b. When your child avoids pornography sites:

   　　a. Verbally reinforce them

   　　b. Apply positive consequences

9. Experience the benefits of recovery

If you have never addressed the pornography situation before with your child, this is an overview of how to approach it. The following chapters flesh out these practices more in-depth.

Not addressing your child's use of internet pornography

Question from a parent: "What will happen if I do not address my child's use of internet pornography? What if I read this book and take no action? What will happen?"

Response: At the least, your child will continue to use internet pornography and masturbate habitually. Your child will continue to struggle with their personal, academic, and professional endeavors. The nature of addiction is progressive, so your child's addiction will tend to worsen. It could be as simple as spending more and more time viewing and consuming internet pornography. It could mean that your child moves to the consumption of more extreme, violent, or taboos forms of high-speed internet pornography. It could also mean that your child could "progress" to more aberrant sexual perversions. If unaddressed, your child could start acting out sexually with prostitutes and possibly unwilling sexual partners. From my experience in the rooms and as a clinician, most people struggling with more severe forms of sex addiction also struggle with compulsive pornography use. As pornography consumption is an escalating behavior,[38] pornography addiction is a gateway to more harmful sex addictions such as viewing child pornography (child abuse imagery), soliciting prostitutes, exhibitionism, or voyeurism.

Often, people struggling with sex addiction find themselves violating the law. Your child's addiction to internet pornography could devolve into them having legal consequences. That is, compulsive use of internet pornography is a form of sexually acting out. If your child habitually acts out by compulsively viewing internet pornography and engaging in manual ejaculation, it is my opinion that it is in your child's best interest for you to compassionately intervene, especially when they live in your home. Weigh the pros and cons of intervening and the pros and cons of not intervening and then make your choice.

Parents seem to have a responsibility to their community and family. Thus, as a parent, you are in a unique position where you can assist your child in overcoming their compulsive use of internet pornography. Follow the steps in this book and your child will be on the right track so that they can experience health and wellbeing. As stated, many times throughout this book, your child has to *want* to recover. If you do choose to actively address your child's habitual pornography use, you can only help your child overcome their struggles through compassion and non-judgment. This may mean that you need to do personal healing work before assisting

---

[38] Park, B. Y., Wilson, G., Berger, J., Christman, M., Reina, B., Bishop, F., ... & Doan, A. P. (2016). Is Internet pornography causing sexual dysfunctions? A review with clinical reports. Behavioral Sciences, 6(3), 17.

Recovery and Authoritative Parenting

your child. With the guidance provided in this book, you can help your child recover from their addiction so they can experience radiant health and wellbeing. With the knowledge contained inside this kind of book and your motivation to make a change, you have what it takes to assist your child in recovery.

Serious problems associated with sexually acting-out include voyeurism, exhibitionism, having sex with an unwilling participant (rape), and having sex using deception and manipulation. For people struggling with these kinds of sex addictions, most of them compulsively similtaniously used internet pornography and masturbated before they developed the latter sex addictions. Their addiction progresses because the pornography that they had become accustomed to no longer did it for them; the "tame" pornography (that vaguely resembles natural, live, real sex) no longer "gets them off". They develop a psychological tolerance to non-taboo forms of internet pornography and in order to fuel the beast associated with their addiction, they have to "up the ante" to experience continued excitement and arousal; in turn, they seek out more extreme forms of aggressive or otherwise perverse pornography. Furthermore, an individual's exploration into violent and otherwise taboo forms of pornography often leads its users to aberrant and sometimes criminal behavior.

By addressing your child's addiction to internet pornography, you are significantly decreasing the likelihood that your child's addiction will develop into a more serious problem. By taking action, you are increasing the likelihood that your child will recover from their psychological dependency on high-speed internet pornography. When intervening, act out of love, unconditional positive regard, and kindness. Control your response to the situation because if you overreact, your child could descend further into the darkness of their addiction.

In this chapter, you learned:

- Recovery is the process where the former user significantly reduces or ideally eliminates the use of the drug or behavior and also significantly improves their living situation.
- In recovery and life in general, connection with oneself and other people is needed for health and wellbeing.
- Participation is a Twelve Steps fellowship program or any similar support group helps the individual experience connection.
- If your child has chronic use of high-speed internet pornography and you do not address it, your child is at high risk for developing a more serious sex addiction, which sometimes involves criminality.
- An individual struggling with an addiction needs honesty, accountability, and motivation in order to recover.
- Authoritative parenting is a child-centered approach to child-rearing that holds high expectations for their child's maturity and behaviors and high responsiveness to the needs of their child; this style of parenting is linked with the best outcomes for children.

- People raised by authoritative parents are better at regulating their emotions, thus, they tend to be more successful than people raised by permissive, neglectful, or authoritarian parents.
- Having house rules allows parents to hold their children accountable and help them learn how to behave, so they can have the greatest likelihood of thriving in life.
- Regularly discussing your family values and the harms of internet pornography increase the likelihood that your child will accept accountability for their internet behaviors.
- Before monitoring and providing accountability for your child's internet activity, inform them beforehand.

Chapter 4
Build a Foundation for Recovery

Moving forward, this section of the book figures that your child regularly visits pornography sites. If you have the courage, compassionately intervening is one of the best things you can do to address your child's regular use of online pornography. Be happy with yourself for wanting to positively impact your child's life as it is a noble endeavor to take steps to help them overcome addiction issues. There are many things that you can do to help your child overcome pornography addiction. When approaching your child about their habitual use of pornography, do the following:

- Be emotionally available to your child
- Listen to child
- Validate your child's feelings
- Openly discuss the harmful nature of pornography portraying sexual objectification, regular use of it, and viable approaches to recovery

When a person suffers from addiction, they have a hard time hearing that there is a problem with their habitual use. If you want to have your child listen to you, address the situation with a desire to understand.

Some parents are not equipped to take this kind of compassionate approach because they have unprocessed trauma or suffering of their own; the situation where their child is psychologically dependent on pornography triggers them to the point where they are unable to non-judgmentally and compassionately address it. If you can compassionately and non-judgmentally address your child's compulsive pornography use, you are in a good position. You should feel very thankful that you can gently talk to your child, so they can get help.

Even better, perhaps, your child has come to your spouse or you for guidance on how to overcome their pornography addiction. If this is the case, this significantly increases the likelihood of a timely recovery for your child because they are communicating that they are interested in taking ownership of their recovery. Furthermore, accountability is one of the largest factors when determining the success of your child's recovery. If a person who uses compulsively is accountable to no one, there is an increased likelihood that they will continue to use. Rarely, if ever, a person struggling with addiction recovers without other people's assistance - either professionals or non-professionals or both.

So, whether you have discovered that your child habitually visits pornography sites or your child has come to you for guidance and advice about how to overcome pornography addiction, accountability is vital in both situations. Recovery requires accountability. Regardless of the addiction, the key to effective accountability is being compassionate, non-judgmental, and wanting to understand. That is why if you are unable to control your response and you react to your child's habitual use of online adult material, then you need more education, understanding, and compassion before actively intervening and assisting in the situation.

Be Kind to Yourself

Love yourself. Take care of yourself. Be compassionate with yourself. As a parent, be mindful of your self-care. Avoid neglecting your own needs. Avoid being a martyr. If you sacrifice your self-care, no one in the situation wins. For you to be the best parent that you can be, regularly engage in self-care. As a parent, it is critically important for you to engage in regular self-care. Binge eating ice cream, binge watching TV, or mindlessly consuming streaming media is not a substitute for real self-care. For the steps and actions revealed in the upcoming chapters to be effective, you must take care of your mind and body.

Self-care is the practice of making your needs a priority. Taking care of your mind and body is indispensable for parents of a child struggling with addiction. As you attempt to provide care for your child's needs during this tumultuous time, the stress you experience can grow to the point where it creates burnout for you. Increased stress can manifest as health symptoms, including depression, anxiety, reduced effectiveness of the immune system, obesity, memory and attention issues, and even cancer. To engage in proper self-care, do some of the following:

- Adhere to a regular sleep schedule
- Eat a nutritious diet
- Take a lunch break
- Go for a walk
- Engage in regular exercise

- Talk to a counselor, therapist, or psychologist
- Ask for and accept help
- Do activities you like doing
- Spend time with people you love
- Care for your mental and physical health
- Join a support group
- Reduce stress in your life
- Practice relaxation skills
- Practice seated meditation
- Take a Yoga class
- Set healthy boundaries with people
- Spend time in nature
- Socialize with your friends
- Limit your time online and on social media
- Clean and organize your home
- When you are experiencing stress, use your coping skills

Taking good care of yourself will improve your ability to care for and guide your child. Suppose you are experiencing negative consequences from the stress created from parenting your addicted child, you will be less effective and competent in decision-making, consistency, encouragement, and overall support to your child. Practicing appropriate self-care also allows you to model the desired behavior to your child. As a parent of your child, you lead by example.

Wise Up

Grow your mind. Educate yourself. Get into the right mindset. Learn about authoritative parenting, addiction, and recovery. No one is going to do this for you. You have to have the initiative yourself. You have already taken a big step by purchasing and reading this book. This book educates parents on how to assist their child in overcoming an addiction to internet pornography. This book contains knowledge, terminology, definitions, approaches, and evidence-based strategies that give you the language that you need to help your child overcome their behavioral addiction. Awareness is always the first step in any process of change. By reading this book thus far, you learned:

- how recovery for your child is possible;
- that connection is the remedy for addiction;
- about the pornography industry and its link to human trafficking;
- what addiction looks like and what recovery is about;
- about harm reduction and abstinence approaches to recovery;
- about the harms associated with the consumption of pornography portraying sexual objectification;
- about the benefits associated with authoritative parenting;
- about the improved outcomes associated with having and following through with fair house rules.

Build a Foundation for Recovery

Great job for getting this far in the book! You are doing great! Keep it up! The rest of the book is dedicated to action steps you need to take to assist in your child's recovery.

Motivation and inspiration to change, telling the truth about oneself, and accountability are needed to recover. If a person does not have one of these elements, it significantly decreases the likelihood that the individual will recover from their compulsive use; it is almost certain that they will stay dependent. Motivation to change can only come from the inside. Trained therapists, clinicians, and other professionals have the skills to inspire motivation within the individual. In time, the individual has to internalize this change to maintain abstinence and live a recovery lifestyle. The individual struggling with addiction is better off by reading literature, attending workshops, and listening to educated people to internalize their need for change.

Telling the truth is very important in recovery. Being honest and truthful is needed so the addicted individual can free themself from the past. If a person struggling with addiction is not truthful in their words and actions, the struggling person will continue their addictive ways. When the individual is telling the truth about themselves, the person is accepting the situation for what it is. Acceptance is needed so that the individual can change their ways. If a person does not acknowledge that they have a problem, the person is unable to change their behaviors and circumstances. Furthermore, telling the truth and being held accountable are related. Being held accountable in recovery is critically important because it helps the individual tell the truth about themselves.

Accountability works best when the person who is holding the other accountable is compassionate and seeks to understand where the other person is coming from. A therapist, a treatment team, a parent, a doctor, a teacher, a sponsor, or a coach, a person who is trustworthy and has the addicted one's best interest in mind, can provide accountability.

Stages of Change

The *Stages of Change* is a theory of psychology assessing an individual's orientation toward acting on a new, healthier behavior. In this model, *change* is a "process involving progress through a series of stages."[39] The Stages of Change include:

- Pre-contemplation
- Contemplation
- Preparation
- Action
- Maintenance
- Relapse

In this model, change occurs slowly. Eventually, using the substance or engaging in the addictive act again or relapsing is part of the recovery process. In the early stages, people often resist change; yet, eventually, they become proactive and commit to modifying their behavior. This model shows that change is rarely easy.

---

[39] Prochaska, J. O., & Velicer, W. F. (1997). The transtheoretical model of health behavior change. *American journal of health promotion, 12*(1), 38-48.

Modifying behavior requires a gradual progression of small steps toward a goal.

Pre-contemplation: This is when the person struggling with addiction is unaware of their problem. Denial and self-imposed ignorance characterize this phase. The individual continues to use and has no thoughts of stopping. The person is in denial about their problem. The individual willfully looks the other way so they can continue to use.

Contemplation: This is when the person struggling with addiction is becoming aware that they have a major problem in their life. The struggling person may change superficial things like use a little bit less or a little less frequently. Ambivalence and cognitive dissonance characterize this stage. The addicted individual starts to realize that addiction is holding them back and is a major obstacle to achieving personal and financial goals. In this stage, they start thinking about change. The person starts to think about change yet does not do anything about it or does very little about it. They continue to use, but they are becoming more aware of the nature of their addiction.

Preparation: This is when the person struggling with addiction prepares to take action on addressing their addiction. Experimenting with small changes and collecting new information characterizes this stage. The struggling person is thinking about how they can overcome addiction. That is, the addicted individual starts to think about going to a treatment center, talking with a therapist, or revealing their addiction problem with supportive people in their life. In this stage, the person prepares for change. The individual may read a book about recovery or perform an internet search on addiction and recovery. The individual realizes that they need to dedicate time and energy toward recovery from addiction.

Taking Action: This is when the person struggling with addiction takes concrete steps toward recovery. Direct action toward the goal characterizes this stage. That is, the individual checks into mental health therapy, starts attending Twelve Steps fellowship meetings, or starts to talk with trusted people in their life about their intention to get and stay clean. Taking action is related to early recovery. In early recovery, the individual primarily focuses on staying clean of their problematic behavior.

Relapse: This is when the person struggling with addiction uses the substance or engages in the addictive act again after having some clean time. Disappointment, frustration, and feelings of failure characterize this stage. Relapse is considered part of the recovery process and should be dealt with compassionately, so it decreases the likelihood that the addicted individual's relapse does not lead to active addiction again. These stages are not necessarily linear. An individual struggling with addiction can go through contemplation, preparation, taking action, and then experience a relapse. From relapse, the user can go back to taking action or go back to pre-contemplation or contemplation. If the individual talks about and processes their use shortly after using, there is an increased likelihood that they will return to the Taking Action stage. If the struggling individual engages in their addictive act and does not process it one way or another, their one-time use can easily take them back into active addiction, where they find themselves back in the precontemplation stage of change.

Maintenance: This is when the individual stabilizes and has experienced success in early recovery. Continuing the new behavior and avoiding temptation characterize this stage. The last stage of the recovery process involves maintenance recovery. A person enters into maintenance recovery as sober life becomes the new norm for them. The recoveree is working on behaviors that contributed to and fueled their addiction. In maintenance recovery, ideally, the person is processing their unresolved issues; by integrating any unprocessed trauma, they are significantly increasing the likelihood that they will stay clean for the long-term. Recovery is a lifelong process.

Maintenance recovery can last for the rest of the individual's life. Furthermore, people in maintenance recovery are still susceptible to using again and relapsing, especially if addictive material is available freely on the internet. Finally, an individual in maintenance recovery is positioned to successfully manage their mental health symptoms and overcome their addiction. In maintenance recovery, the individual can use their recovery to fuel their ascent to new heights. The individual has the option to give back to the recovery movement and can serve as a sponsor for a person or two who are in early recovery. In the Twelve Steps program, this is the Twelfth Step. At this point, the recoveree has the option to move into the personal development stage of life, which seems to be less common; but it does happen. It is what happened to me.

Personal Development: This is when the individual dedicates their life to continual self-improvement. Even though personal development usually is not included in the traditional stages of change, I hypothesize that this is an added step in the stages of change in the recovery process. This is what happened to me. And I see this more and more online - recovery-oriented personal development. I used my recovery from substance abuse to be a catalyst for my personal development and the awakening of my entrepreneurial spirit. I see my past substance abuse and pornography addiction as a blessing, as it has helped fuel my practice of mastery.

The Power of Your Subconscious Mind

Have perspective. Have faith that it is not over. Remember, good things can come out of addiction. You can help bring that about in your child. There is balance in the Universe. There are actions and reactions. The Universe is an intentional place. In one study, researchers found that recovering individuals have statistically higher levels of faith and spirituality than those continuing to relapse; also, those relapsing individuals show significantly lower levels of spirituality than those in recovery.[40] Furthermore, create it in your mind that you help your child recover, i.e., see it in your mind that your child recovers. Visualize your child living their best life and feel it. Conjure up the emotions of joy and contentment. What does your child's best life look like? When your eyes are closed, see it in the space between your eyebrows. Have faith that your child wants to live their best life in the intentional Universe that we are part of. Suffering is not humanity's original state of consciousness. Our natural state of awareness is happiness and joy. To restore your child's ability to experience true

---

[40] Jarusiewicz, B. (2000). Spirituality and addiction: Relationship to recovery and relapse. *Alcoholism Treatment Quarterly*, *18*(4), 99-109.

Build a Foundation for Recovery

happiness and joy, they must liberate themself from the shackles of pornography addiction.

Connect with your intuition. Learn to flow with the Universe. Remember, there is a universe inside of you. To change the outer world "outside of yourself," change your inner world. You got it! You can do it. This is the journey for all of us. The path of self-healing! Remember, all life is connected. Everything happens for a reason. The Universe was created intentionally. People struggling with addiction benefit from taking a leap of faith. *Faith* is a conviction or trust in a person or thing. For example, trusting someone involves having faith in the idea that what they are saying is true. Faith is when a person believes in something that does not require logical proof for material evidence. Faith is when people decide to believe in something greater than their ego. Have faith that there is an Intelligence behind the "physical" Universe.

Realize the power of beliefs. Your subconscious mind can enslave or liberate you. To recover more quickly, an addicted individual needs to let go of the subconscious beliefs that do not serve them and adopt new, constructive beliefs. This is a conscious process. An individual can use their conscious mind to de-program and re-program their subconscious mind. This is an in-depth process, but it is worth it. It makes the rest of the recovery process a whole lot easier. If a person in recovery becomes proficient at shaping their subconscious mind, they are bound to recover and live their best life. The subconscious mind is the part of the mind that is larger and more powerful than the conscious mind. Most of our actions come from the subconscious mind, and the conscious mind fine-tunes those behaviors. If a person wants to change their behaviors much more easily, they need to de-program and re-program their subconscious mind.

De-program and re-program your subconscious mind and consider teaching your child how to do the same. There are whole books written on this topic, so this is a very brief overview of how to de-program and re-program your subconscious mind. De-programming one's subconscious mind is an in-depth process, because forces outside our control strongly condition many people in modern society. Many people of the mainstream are conditioned and programmed via governments, corporations, media, advertisements, TV programming, extremist religions, etc. Furthermore, the pornography industry has mainstreamed violent pornography; they have *pornified* mainstream culture. We can do better as a society.

Most people have not consciously programmed their subconscious mind; they have given this power away to an authority that does not care about them. Governmental and otherwise corporate institutions condition people to behave in such ways that benefit the conditioning entities. When corporations and bureaucracies completely indoctrinate an individual to be nothing more than a consumer who avoids critical thought, they become highly susceptible to addiction. As internet pornography is accessible, anonymous, and affordable, the programmed individual is susceptible to developing an addiction to internet pornography. When people are dependent upon drugs or a behavioral addiction such as gambling or pornography addiction, they are easier to control by those who aim to control them. When the

Build a Foundation for Recovery

masses are dependent upon something destructive such as pornography portraying objectification and commodification, bureaucratic institutions benefit because individuals struggling with addiction do not oppose their corrupt corporatist systems and they do not strive to live their best life. Individuals mired in addiction are too focused on feeding their habit than consciously living the good life.

To guarantee recovery from an addiction, an addicted individual needs to de-program and re-program their subconscious mind, and this does not necessarily need to be done one after the other. They can be done simultaneously. De-programming needs to occur because when a new belief is imposed on the mind and the old belief is still neurologically imprinted in the brain, the two beliefs contradict each other, so the individual experiences cognitive dissonance. The belief that is more myelinated in the brain circuitry will be the one issuing the commands to the conscious mind; whatever belief has been accessed more frequently and with a longer duration is the belief that will win out. In my view, it takes 30 to 90 days to learn a new behavior; and it requires daily input. For the new belief to take root and bubble up to the conscious mind, the individual needs to let go of old beliefs that do not serve them. The following can be done to de-program your subconscious mind:

- Process any unresolved trauma or suffering
- Consider receiving Eye Movement Desensitization and Reprocessing (EMDR) or another form of trauma-responsive therapy

- Stop giving your power away to illegitimate forms of authority
- Question advertisements and propaganda that is disseminated by governments, corporations, and the media
- Question conformity, consumerism, commodification, and bureaucracies
- Avoid relying on religious dogma, clergy, ideologies, bureaucrats, etc
- Minimize or avoid identification with materialism
- Look within yourself
- Be conscious of what you allow into your senses
- Be mindful of the kind of foods you consume
- Consciously choose your sources of news and information
- Develop mindfulness and learn to meditate
- Learn to practice Clinical EFT[41,42,43] on yourself

Use your subconscious mind to overcome the situation and consider teaching your child how to use their subconscious mind to make things easier on themselves. One way to modify your subconscious mind is by presenting it with different associations. If you feel upset,

---

[41] Church, D. (2013). Clinical EFT as an evidence-based practice for the treatment of psychological and physiological conditions. *Psychology, 4*(08), 645.

[42] Church, D., & Marohn, S. (2013). *Clinical EFT Handbook* (Vol. 1). Hay House, Inc.

[43] Bennett, M. (n.d.). *A Pocket Guide to EFT* [Pamphlet].

practice deep breathing. Write down your intention. Write, "If I feel upset, I practice deep breathing." Change the associations through repetition; through affirmations and other techniques like neuro-linguistic programming, your subconscious mind can start working for your child and you.

For new programming of the mind to take root, release the conditioning that may have been programmed into your mind. The subconscious mind is like the auto-pilot feature of an airplane; it has been pre-programmed to follow a specific route, and the individual is unable to deviate from the pre-programmed route unless they change the directions of the subconscious mind. The following can be done to re-program your subconscious mind and install empowering beliefs:

- Seek truth, beauty, and love within
- Decide in your mind what kind of life you intend to live
- Commit to living your best life
- Focus on what you like and are grateful for
- Read books or audiobooks that expand your mind and empower you
- Adopt empowering beliefs
- Find and write affirmations
- Emotionally recite your affirmations daily
- Regularly think about and visualize living your best life

- Express yourself creatively
- Learn to speak your mind and your truth
- Meditate, meditate, meditate

I go as far as writing affirmations, recording them electronically, and looping the audio file over and over again while I am sleeping. This process allows the audio affirmations to bypass my conscious mind and the positive statements get imprinted directly into my subconscious mind. Listening to audio affirmations at a low level while you sleep is a very effective way to implant new, empowering beliefs into one's mind. Once I started using this technique, I have continued to use it because the results that are produced by this technique are incredible. If you want your child or you to have a much easier time changing behaviors, de-program and re-program your subconscious mind. It takes work and dedication; but, it is worth it. You are worth it. Your child is worth it. It could be the most profound journey that your child and you embark upon. I know it has been for me.

Spend Quality Time

Strengthen your relationship with your child. Spend quality time with them. Schedule recurring quality family time with your child. Quality time together communicates to your child that you care about them. Spending quality time with your child is beneficial to your child's development and happiness. Quality time is when you give your undivided attention to your child, even if it is for only one hour each week; hopefully, it is more than that. That means to avoid checking email, checking your

Build a Foundation for Recovery

phone, or talking with a friend. Quality time can be spent doing something your child likes doing. Even something as simple as sitting down with your child and family to eat dinner, not talking about work, and being present with your child serves as quality time. Examples of activities that your child and you can do together:

- Go hiking
- Walk the dog
- Go jogging
- Play a video game that avoids violence, etc.,
- Play the basketball game H-O-R-S-E
- Play a board or card game
- Put a puzzle together
- Ride bikes together
- Volunteer together
- Browse a bookstore or the library together
- Take a road trip together
- Visit a park
- Register and jog a fun run 5K
- Go to a free or low-cost museum
- Go on a walking tour of your local city
- Gaze at the stars at night time or at a Planetarium
- Perform a random act of kindness together

Teach your child the importance of equality among all people of society and reinforce this. Talk with your child about how all people are equal. Model this behavior. Model giving respect and dignity to all people. In summary, the benefits of spending quality time with your adolescent include increased compliance with your requests and expectations, improved mental and physical health for parents and child, and increased empathy and understanding of your child.

Teenagers can be hesitant to spend quality time with their parents because they might think it is uncool. Be persistent with your child in finding time to spend together. Even if your child is at first resistant to your motions toward spending time together, give them space, then shortly, motion to schedule quality time again. Talk to your child indirectly about the benefits of spending quality time together. Consider talking to them in an indirect manner such as: when driving, preparing the dinner table, or washing dishes. It might be a little bit easier for your child to listen to you if you do not engage in direct eye contact with them. Your child might be able to hear you a little bit more while engaged in a conversation that is not so face-to-face. Try a combination of the two. Find out what works for your child.

Educate Your Child

When you have one of your ongoing heart-to-heart conversations about pornography with your child, educate them on matters related to pornography, addiction, and internet rules. When having the conversation or ideally the ongoing conversation about pornography, be educated on what pornography consists of in the 2010s and beyond. As long as your adolescent is mature enough, educate them on the nature of pornography and its industry; to get the conversation started, you have everything you need in this book. That is why I spelled it out. If your adolescent is near the age of 15 or 16 or older, consider explaining that the modern pornography industry manufactures and disseminates pornographic content that portrays:

- The sexual objectification of women
    - A woman is merely an object of sexual pleasure, nothing more.
    - A woman's only purpose is to serve as a sexual object for a man.
- The commodification of women
    - A woman is a commercial product that can be bought and sold.
    - Access to a woman's body is a commodity that involves supply and demand.
- Misogyny (a hatred of women)
    - Men physically and psychologically abusing women.
    - Men slapping, hitting, and spitting on women.
    - Women do not have minds for thinking; women have bodies to have sex with.
- The humiliation, degradation, and powerlessness of the feminine
    - A man anally penetrates a woman and then directly inserts his penis into her mouth without cleaning off his penis.

- A man or multiple men ejaculating on the face of a woman, while she acts as if she likes it.
- A man choking a woman, while violently penetrating her.
- Two men simultaneously penetrating the same woman.
- Multiple men having sex with the same woman, i.e. gangbang.

- Racism
  - A muscular black man with a very large penis forcefully penetrating a Barbie-doll looking, white woman.
  - Women of color are more often portrayed as the object of abuse in aggressive pornography.

Consider explaining how pornography's casual portrayal of abuse tends to normalize violence toward women. Explain how viewing pornography that shows objectification, commodification, misogyny, and degradation of women is harmful; and this conditions its viewers to accept the debasement of women and the feminine gender. Explain how this is not okay and how it violates your family's core values. If you need to, read parts of this text out loud to your adolescent. Let them read this book.

You may think some of these examples of modern pornography are extreme, and they are. At the same time, the hardcore pornography of the 2010s and beyond is not

Build a Foundation for Recovery

the same as the hardcore pornography of the 1990s. Modern hardcore pornography portrays body-punishing sexual acts; pornography portrays aggression and violence toward women. In the modern pornography industry, now mainstream niches include:

- A man gagging a woman with his penis until she vomits.
- A man urinating on the face of a woman.
- A man calling a woman a "bitch, whore, slut, cunt."

There is a real likelihood that your adolescent has viewed this kind of pornography. Pornography portraying these kinds of violent content is the kind of videos that get algorithmically ranked on the top of "free" tube-style sites such as PornHub, xVideos, and xHampster.

Honesty, Accountability, and Motivation

Educate your child about what they need to do to recover from the habitual use of pornography. As previously stated, motivation to change, honesty and transparency, and accountability are the three elements required for a person to overcome addiction. Once trust is built more fully in your relationship with your child, educate your child on what is needed to overcome their addiction to internet pornography.

Motivation and inspiration to change is something that can waver. Some days, the individual might be very motivated to change; yet, some days, the individual may not experience any motivation or low motivation to change their behaviors. Consuming and digesting inspirational literature and media is a wise choice for your child. There are many motivational and inspirational books, literature, and media that specialize in motivating your adolescent to adopt constructive habits.

One of the teachers that I follow, Zig Ziglar, states that "People often say that motivation doesn't last. Well, neither does bathing, that's why we recommend it daily." To me, this means motivation is like taking a bath; we need to do it every day. This quote means that motivation and inspiration to change sometimes can be a transient force in the individual's experience. If the individual wants to maximize their opportunity to overcome compulsive use, it is in the person's best interest to expose themselves to inspirational literature on a regular, if not daily basis. This can be devotional literature that is read in the morning or on smartphone apps that can provide motivation and strength to change unfruitful behaviors.

Encourage your adolescent to see that honesty and transparency are needed to recover from pornography addiction. Honesty and transparency can manifest itself in a variety of ways. One of the best ways to be honest and transparent about one's addiction is through participation in a Twelve Steps fellowship program such as Alcoholics Anonymous (AA), Sex and Love Addicts Anonymous (SLAA), or Porn Addicts Anonymous (PAA). There are also resources such as the NoFap community where your adolescent can communicate with other individuals who are working to overcome their compulsive use of pornography. I have had a few experiences connecting with accountability partners via NoFap, and it has been a wonderful experience for my recovery. My interactions and connection with my accountability partner have been key in my recovery.

The third element that is required to recover from any addiction involves accountability. That is, the second and third elements are very closely related. Accountability means that the person is held accountable for their actions. If and when the recovering individual uses after some clean time, the recoveree has to address that with the person who is holding them accountable. If the recovering individual stays clean, they receive praise from the individual or organization that is providing accountability. An accountability partner or a Twelve Steps sponsor is one of the key ways that an individual can find accountability for their use of pornography. If your adolescent is considering participating in a Twelve Steps group and finding a sponsor, it is best to figure out what kind of sponsor your adolescent is looking for. A Twelve Steps sponsor is a very valuable resource, as sponsors are people who intimately know about addiction and recovery. If your adolescent decides to attend Twelve Steps meetings, they need to be safe when interacting with the general public.

If your adolescent does choose a sponsor, they need to be compassionate and non-judgmental to your child's struggles. If your child is interested in following the Twelve Steps approach to recovery, coach your child on what characteristics to look for in a sponsor. Help your child to come up with a list of characteristics that they would like to find in a sponsor. Here is a list of examples:

- My sponsor is the same sex as me.

- My sponsor has at least 3 - 5 years clean from compulsive use of internet pornography, sexually acting out, or other bottom-line behaviors.
- I can learn from my sponsor.
- I like listening to my sponsor.
- My sponsor has enough time to dedicate to my needs and preferences.
- My sponsor has what I want.

Sponsorship is one of the best ways to experience accountability in recovery. When you are using one of the accountability software programs that are discussed in the next chapter, you will be able to link the accountability software with one or more email addresses. The people receiving the email see a report from the software that includes internet search words and internet sites visited by your child.

Educate your child on their options for recovery. After you have educated your child on what is needed to recover, the next step involves educating your child on their options for recovery. Options include participation in a Twelve Steps program such as SLAA, engaging in mental health therapy, or being accountable to an accountability partner, a Twelve Step sponsor, or you as their parent. One of these options or a combination of multiple elements will put your child in the best position to recover from pornography dependency. Explaining the benefits of individual therapy will increase the likelihood that your child will be interested in engaging in therapy. Therapy involves the integration of unprocessed emotions. Once a person processes their past trauma or suffering, cognitive resources in the person's mind are freed up. This allows the person to be more fully engaged in the present moment, and the present moment is where the magic of life exists.

A complement to recovery from compulsive pornography use involves the regular practice of mindfulness and meditation. The practice of meditation involves sitting in silence; concentration meditation involves focusing on the breath or focusing on one thing to decrease the likelihood that disruptive thoughts come up in the present moment. The practice of meditation is a very powerful approach when working to overcome any addiction. I have personal experience with practicing seated meditation since late 2011, and it is one of the key practices that has allowed me to overcome my compulsive use of substances and internet pornography. Once you have educated your child on their options for recovery, you all are in a position to explore their triggers and coping skills. As part of mental health therapy, your adolescent's clinician will help them establish meaningful, objective goals as part of your child's treatment plan. You can also assist your child in formulating their treatment goals.

Listen and Then Discuss

Listen to and seek to understand your child. Be sensitive and recognize how difficult and embarrassing it may be for your child to face up to their struggles with pornography use. Identify your child's regular use of internet pornography as a situation that needs to be addressed. Reflect on how it feels when you are overwhelmed, and your child's emotions seem to be spinning out of control. Understand how shame can indirectly influence your child to behave in ways that they will regret later. Here are some tips related to holding space for your adolescent child:

- Turn off your parent alarm
- Control your reactions to your child's behavior
- Listen without judgment or reaction
- Avoid catastrophic, black and white, all or nothing thinking
- Avoid over empathizing, dramatizing your emotions
- Ask open questions like "Can you tell me more about that?", "I hear you say this, can you tell me a little bit more about what you mean?"

Further, validate your child's feelings. Validating your child's feelings is going to help build trust with them. Validating your child's feelings allows them to realize that you are truly listening to them and that they are not being judged for consuming internet pornography. When you validate your child's feelings, their confidence grows just a little bit and allows them to gain strength that they did not realize that they once had. The little bit of strength that your child uncovered allows them to move into the action stage of recovery.

Validating your child's feelings gives them motivation and inspiration to change. When you validate your child's feelings, it takes a lot of pressure off them. By validating your child's feelings, they realize that they are being listened to, and it removes a sense of isolation that is

Build a Foundation for Recovery

experienced by people struggling with addiction. Validating your child's feelings and emotions allows them to move from contemplation to preparation to action. Examples of how to validate your child's experience include:

- Avoid lecturing your adolescent
- When your adolescent asks to talk about sensitive matters, seize the moment
- If you can, make yourself available to them right then and there
- Consciously respond to what your adolescent is talking about
- Summarize what your adolescent has expressed
- Say, "If I was experiencing that, I would feel that way too."
- Say "I hear you say this, is that what you mean?"
- Make eye contact, nod head in a gentle way, and say, "I see."

Validating your child's feelings and perspective allows them to share thoughts and feelings without you judging, criticizing, ridiculing, or abandoning them. By validating your child, you allow them to feel heard and understood. You communicate that you love and accept your child no matter what they are feeling or thinking. Now that you have set a solid foundation of how you will approach your child's dependency on internet pornography, next, you will take action.

In this chapter, you learned:

- Self-care involves having a routine where an individual maintains one's health and well-being.
- Before discussing with your child, be aware of the pornography industry, the harms associated with compulsive pornography use, and that recovery is achievable.
- Pre-contemplation, contemplation, preparation, action, relapse, and maintenance are the Stages of Change.
- Just as the Twelve Steps teach, having faith and surrendering to a higher power will give your child strength over their uncontrollable habit.
- Harnessing the power of your child's and your subconscious mind will give your child the highest likelihood of recovery.
- Reciting affirmations, listening to affirmations, and practicing creative visualization can help your child and you to reprogram your subconscious mind.
- Spending quality time with your child is conducive to their development and it allows you to impress upon your child - values of health, well-being, and success.
- Educate your child about the harms associated with the regular use of internet pornography and their options for recovery; this helps build a foundation that will allow your child to modify their behavior.

- If your child is around the age of 16 and needs the motivation to change, educate them about sex objectification, misogyny, and degradation.
- By listening to your child and validating their feelings, you are giving your child the space they need to talk about why they are sexually acting out.

Chapter 5
Take Action for Recovery

Authoritative Parenting

As mentioned, authoritative parenting is a parenting style characterized by high responsiveness to the child's needs while having high expectations of their behaviors. Parents employing the authoritative style set limits on their child's behavior and are very consistent in enforcing boundaries and applying consequences to behavior. Implementing an authoritative style of parenting allows you to have a say in what goes on in your household. Employing strategies and methods associated with authoritative parenting allows you to run a much smoother household. When you are parenting authoritatively, you will have much greater peace of mind. It may take some getting used to. If you are interested in having a peaceful state of mind, parent authoritatively. By parenting authoritatively, you are teaching your child skills they need to learn to successfully support themselves.

Identify Triggers

Help your child identify triggers that lead to them to using pornography. *Triggers* can be defined as certain people, places, or things serving as a sensory cue to the individual's mind that create an urge where they want to use their drug or behavior of choice. As modern-day culture is infused with hypersexuality and advertisements using sex to sell products and services, triggers for pornography use appearing on the internet are ubiquitous; they are practically everywhere. Triggers for pornography use exist in so many places because of the perception that "sex sells." Using the internet itself can be a major trigger for people struggling with pornography addiction because much of the internet portrays women who are scantily-clothed. This can be easily found on sites such as YouTube and many other modern news agency outlets. Examples of potential triggers:

- Feelings of hunger or tiredness
- Feelings of loneliness or social isolation
- Feelings of anger or aggression
- Feelings of disappointment or grief
- Feelings of shame, guilt, or unworthiness
- Feelings of hurt, sadness, depression, or misery
- Sexy pictures on the internet or other forms of media such as TV
- Certain people, locations, places, or smells
- Experiences of overwhelming stress
- Overconfidence
- Sex and romantic relationships

Just using the internet can be triggering for people dependent on digital pornography. Once you have recognized that your child habitually visits pornography sites, their therapist will help identify their triggers. If your child does not have a therapist, you can assist your child in identifying their triggers; at the same time, consider getting a therapist to do this with your child. Consider saying, "Think back to when you would use pornography. What was happening in your environment or your head before you used pornography? Were you feeling lonely and then would use porn? Would you become upset with someone in your life and then use? Would you get stressed out and then use?" It is best to use open-ended questions, but the latter can be helpful to stimulate thought. You help your child recognize the *antecedent*, the stimulus that is experienced prior to the behavior of using internet pornography. Helping your child identify their triggers will decrease exposure to pornography and they can learn how to deal effectively with their triggers. For coping skills to be fully effective, have your child become aware of their triggers for pornography use.

Utilize Coping Skills

Stress reduction *coping skills* are strategies and approaches, thought patterns, and behaviors that a person can engage in to avoid compulsive use. Coping skills involve a range of thought patterns and behaviors. From my years of professional experience as an addiction therapist, I have identified two categories of effective coping skills. The first category of coping skills involves processing emotions. This includes talking with a trusted, non-judgmental person, journaling, talking into an audio recorder, or engaging in some form of somatic therapy. *Somatic therapy* is a form of body-centered holistic therapy that aims to restore connection and healing between the mind and the body. In somatic forms of trauma healing, the individual engages in mind-body exercises that release stuck energy in the body. If your child comes to you when they have an urge to use, first thank them for seeking out your assistance. Then, ask your child:

- How long have you been feeling that way?
- What was happening before you started feeling that way?
- What can I do to help you?
- What can you do to avoid use in this situation?

Then, actively listen to your child from there. Another coping skill involving the processing of their emotions is journaling about the person's perceptions, sensations, and emotions. As they are occurring in the present moment, your child will write down their feelings and what is going on in their head. By doing so, your child will be engaging in the cathartic process; they will tend to release stuck energy from their body.

Catharsis is a process where the individual talks or journals and does not constrict themselves with what they are saying. The person just talks about what they are experiencing; it is a process of clearing and cleansing one's emotional state. Catharsis can also be done through creatively expressing oneself. The cathartic process allows a person to release whatever emotion they are experiencing and can make it possible for an individual to significantly increase the likelihood that they will behave according to their recovery. Further, mindfulness-based body movement practices, namely Yoga and Tai Chi, are another set of coping skills that help the individual to process their emotions. Practicing Yoga asana (the postures) or Tai Chi allows the individual to subtly process past trauma. Practicing Yoga or Tai Chi can be used in the present moment to process and integrate your child's and your emotions.

Yin Yoga is a slower form of Yoga asana where the individual puts themselves in a position for an extended period. Practicing Yin Yoga effectively helps the person to process their emotions. Yin Yoga has similarities to seated meditation, as the Yin and Restorative Yoga postures are held for minutes at a time. When practicing Yin and Restorative forms of Yoga asana, the practitioner activates the *parasympathetic nervous system*, which induces a state of relaxation for the individual. That is, one category of effective coping skills involves the processing of emotions in the present moment. Talking with a trusted person (such as a mental health counselor in individual therapy, an available friend, or a sponsor), journaling, practicing breathwork, or practicing Yoga or Tai Chi are various examples that allow the individual to process their emotions in the present moment.

Bilateral stimulation exercises, namely the butterfly hug is another way to process emotions in the present moment. *Bilateral stimulation* refers to stimuli that occur in a rhythmic pattern that alternates between the right and left sides of the body.[44] The alternating stimulation of the body sends signals to both hemispheres of the brain, meaning that the left and right side of the brain is activated at the same time. When both sides of the brain are stimulated simultaneously, the individual is much more equipped to process their emotions. Bilateral stimulation is an element of Eye Movement

---

[44] Grant, M. (n.d.). What is Bilateral Stimulation? Retrieved November 12, 2020, from https://anxietyreleaseapp.com/what-is-bilateral-stimulation/

Desensitization and Reprocessing (EMDR). Further, EMDR is a powerful therapeutic technique that has years of empirical research demonstrating its clinical efficacy; EMDR is very effective for treating anxiety-based mental health symptoms.[45] In a similar way to that of the butterfly hug, Emotional Freedom Techniques can be used to help an individual reduce anxiety in the present moment.[46] Conclusively, the first category of coping skills involves catharsis or somatic techniques.

The second category of effective coping skills involves distraction techniques. There are many more forms of distraction-based coping skills, then compared to those that process emotions. The coping skills allowing for the processing of emotions are the gold standard for overcoming addiction, but distraction-based coping skills are effective in allowing the person to stay free of compulsive use. There are many more types of distraction-based coping skills. Some distraction-based coping skills include listening to music, watching a favorite TV show or streaming media, coloring in an adult coloring book, and walking outside. Walking outside may be more of a somatic technique, but I think this is more of a question for science.

Coping skills are critically important to a recovering individual. In recovery, coping skills are not the end-all-be-all though. If a person has unresolved trauma

---

[45] Shapiro, F., & Solomon, R. M. (2010). Eye movement desensitization and reprocessing. *The Corsini encyclopedia of psychology*, 1-3.

[46] Bach, D., Groesbeck, G., Stapleton, P., Sims, R., Blickheuser, K., & Church, D. (2019). Clinical EFT (Emotional Freedom Techniques) improves multiple physiological markers of health. *Journal of evidence-based integrative medicine*, *24*, 2515690X18823691.

in the past, the individual needs to process their emotions to effectively overcome pornography addiction. If an individual does not process their unresolved suffering or trauma, the individual might be able to stay clean for an extended time. However, the person will need to over-utilize coping skills to the point where they still experience daily struggles. If your child has any unresolved trauma, your child will greatly benefit from processing it. The processing of emotions and the resolution of outstanding trauma is called for in long-term recovery, if the individual thus chooses. When it comes to light that your adolescent has a problem with the use of pornography and is interested in recovery, your child must first identify their triggers and immediately start using coping skills.

Stabilization is needed in recovery, and coping skills that are regularly used provide security for the individual. Using coping skills allows the individual to start significantly reducing their use, but over time the individual's willpower can break down. This is another reason why honesty and accountability are critically important when in recovery. Coping skills are individualized for each person, so your child needs to identify and use coping skills that work for them. Giving your child a list of effective coping skills will allow them to identify emotional regulation strategies that work for them. Of course, your child needs to ask permission prior to leaving the house or making plans outside the home. Examples of coping skills:

- Be with a supportive person
- Call and talk with a friend

- Call my sponsor
- Chew gum
- Clean up trash on your street or in a public park
- Clean your apartment/house
- Color in an adult coloring book
- Cook a healthy meal or make a smoothie
- Decorate your mirror with positive affirmations
- Do aromatherapy - candle, lotion, essential oils, room spray
- Do deep breathing
- Do EFT tapping
- Do exercises
- Do the butterfly hug
- Draw or doodle
- Find new music online on video-sharing websites
- Go outside, listen and observe nature
- Go to a public place such as a park, grocery store, or library
- Hug someone
- Let yourself cry
- Listen to an inspirational speech on a video-sharing website
- Listen to a self-help/personal development audiobook

- Listen to some of your favorite music
- Make a gratitude list
- Make a list of blessings in your life
- Make plans with a friend and mark it on your calendar
- Manage your time, practice time management
- Organize and declutter your bedroom
- Paint a painting, even if it is an abstract painting
- Perform a random act of kindness for someone
- Pet a cat or dog
- Plant seeds for a plant
- Play a board game, chess, perhaps online
- Play a video game, perhaps online
- Post a positive post on social media
- Practice creative, emotional visualization
- Practice sitting meditation
- Practice Yoga postures
- Pray to your higher power
- Punch a punching bag
- Put a puzzle together
- Read a book or novel
- Read the Bible, Yoga Sutras, or other sacred text
- Read Wikipedia

- Read your Twelve Steps manual/big book
- Recite the Serenity Prayer
- Ride your bicycle
- Rip paper into small pieces of paper
- Run or jog
- Say out loud things you are thankful for
- Sew, knit, or crochet
- Shoot basketball
- Sit in the sun
- Smile at the next handful of people that you come across
- Squeeze a stress ball
- Start of a collection of something you like
- Stretch your body
- Study and practice Feng Shui
- Suck on a peppermint
- Take a hot or cold shower
- Take a warm bath
- Take photographs of nature
- Talk into an audio recorder and reflect
- Text a friend and tell them one thing you like about them
- Turn on dance music and dance

- Vacuum a room or two in your living space
- Visit an animal shelter
- Walk outside or on a track
- Watch a movie
- Work in the garden
- Work on completing items on your to-do list
- Write a letter or send an email to a friend
- Write down 3 things you are grateful for
- Write down an inspirational quote in your notebook
- Write down your daily, weekly, monthly goals
- Write down your to-do list
- Write in a journal
- Write out a description of your dream car
- Write out a description of your dream house
- Write out a description of your dream job
- Write out a description of your dream partner
- Write yourself an "I love you because…" letter

There are many different kinds of coping skills. Find a set of coping skills that work for your child and you and when you are stressed out, do them. Even if you think you cannot do it, you have to do it. You have to learn a new way. If you have to, force yourself to look at a list of coping skills and pick one and do it.

With the assistance of a trained therapist, a support group, or an accountability partner, your child can learn how to use coping skills when they have an urge to use internet pornography. When your child uses their coping skills and avoids use, this is a good opportunity for them to receive a small reward for avoiding use. For example, your child comes to you when they were triggered to use. So, your child processed their emotions with you, and then your child was able to stay clean. That evening after dinner, you treat your child to soft-serve ice cream or something along those lines. Say, "I am getting you this ice cream tonight for staying clean earlier today. In the future, you will not have me to reward you with an incentive. You need to learn that when you stay free of pornography use, that you are healthier in your mind and body and you maintain healthier relationships with other people. Do you know what I mean?" Listen to your child's response and work to understand their point of view. In summary, the identification of triggers and utilization of coping skills is a crucial step that is needed to take place in your child's recovery from pornography dependency.

Be A Benevolent Ruler

Figure out what privileges you give your child. *Privileges* are things you allow your child to experience that go beyond taking care of their material and emotional needs. Communicate your child's privileges to them. Inform your child that their access to rewards is contingent upon good behavior. Your child only gets certain rewards for behaving appropriately. Establish family and internet rules. Hold your child accountable for their behaviors. Be compassionate. Enforce the rules. When your child violates the agreed-upon rule, address the situation, and consider having your child do time-out or removing a privilege such as decreasing screen time from 60 to 45 minutes a day for three days.

Teach your child that it is your responsibility to instill in them behaviors that are aligned with success. Encourage your child to do better. If you are able and can still maintain healthy boundaries, build your child up. If you see it as meaningful, inspire hope in your child. Further, set clear expectations and boundaries on your child's behavior. Setting and keeping boundaries with your child is critically important for them to internalize the motivation needed to change. Your boundaries are limitations on your behavior. Your boundaries are the things that you will and will not do for your child. Your boundaries serve as reasonable ways for your child to treat you and for you to treat your child. People struggling with addiction are notorious for testing and violating boundaries with those they love and care about. Think about the kinds of behaviors you will accept and those that you will not accept. Set boundaries with your child when things are peaceful.

When your dependent child tests your boundaries, setting clear limitations will help you maintain consistency in your application of consequences; it will help you to consistently apply consequences to their desired and undesired behaviors. To have clear boundaries with your child, consider the following:

- Are you willing to sacrifice your needs for the desires of your child?

- What level of internet pornography use are you willing to accept, if any?
- How do you expect to be treated by your child?
- Are you enabling your child's use of internet pornography?
- Besides talking to your child about their relapse, do you plan on removing any of their privileges? If so, which ones and for how long?

Setting clear boundaries helps to clarify the distinction between helping your child and enabling your child's addictive behavior. Enabling compulsive behavior is a sign of poor boundaries. A parent enabling their addicted child will make excuses, blame themselves, focus on reducing short-term pain, and unintentionally reinforcing addictive behaviors. Setting clear boundaries may increase disagreements in the short-term, but it demonstrates to your child that you will not be manipulated by their brain disease.

One could even argue that when the parent provides housing and internet access to their child who is dependent on pornography and does nothing to address the situation, the parent is enabling their child to remain dependent on it. If you have not already, identify your child's privileges. Examples of privileges include:

- Have screen time
- Have more than 15 minutes a day of screen time
- Possess a smartphone
- Have a cookie after dinner

- Play their favorite game or video game
- Have an extra hang out session with a friend for the week
- Receive a nice pair of shoes, as compared to the generic, utilitarian model
- Pick which restaurant to attend
- Have extended outdoor recreation
- Drive the car to a social event
- Go on a date with a peer
- Stay up late without adult supervision

In parenting, privileges are age-dependent. As your child develops, you have to keep updating your child's list of privileges. When applying consequences for behavior, it is best to employ the least restrictive form of removing privileges. If your child can learn from a time-out session of 10 minutes, there is no need to have your child sit in time-out for 25 minutes. Same with reducing screen time. If your child can learn from reducing their screen time from 60 minutes a day to 45 minutes a day for three days, there is no need to apply a more restrictive consequence. If your child simply learns by addressing the situation with them, do that; in this situation, there is no need to remove privileges because they are learning and have a close connection with their parent or parents. That is, simply by talking to your child about their continued use of internet pornography, your child is likely to experience guilt; this is natural. This bad feeling is present for a reason; it serves an evolutionary purpose to motivate the individual to modify their behavior, so they do not have to experience guilt again.

Have Internet Rules

Creating and enforcing reasonable rules is critically important in helping your child recover from their addiction because it sets clear expectations governing their behavior. It is the parents' responsibility to teach their child about sound decision-making. Creating and enforcing reasonable rules helps your child learn appropriate behaviors, which sets them up for success. Having a way to enforce the rules is important as well. Checking the history and using safe browsing searches via accountability software is one way that the parent can work to hold their child accountable for their online behaviors and thus keep their child safe. Conclusively, having internet rules is about keeping your child safe and setting up them for success.

Creating specific rules around internet use for your children is a personal preference. In this text, I list various rules and guidelines that you can use to help create rules for your family. If you have a partner, discuss with them which rules are appropriate for your child. The rules listed here are merely some suggestions, and you probably may benefit from customizing the language to fit your particular take on parenting. Authoritative parenting is correlated with the best outcomes for raising a child. The internet rules are expectations, and when the expectations are not met, there are natural consequences associated with violating the rules. I do not advocate punitive consequences associated with breaking the rules. If and when your child does relapse on internet pornography, their use needs to be addressed in order for them to make progress in recovery.

As I have served as an addiction therapist for years in the Greater Cincinnati area, I have plenty of experience compassionately and non-judgmentally holding individuals accountable for their behavior. When a person compassionately holds another accountable for compulsive use, the recoveree is given the space that they need to reflect on the experience. This allows the recovering person to feel the emotions that are associated with the relapse. When the individual feels the guilt that is often accompanied by a relapse, it can be a major motivating force for them to stay clean in the future. The bad feeling resulting from a relapse serves as an evolutionary purpose, which can motivate the individual in the future to choose a constructive behavior.

Accountability software such as Covenant Eyes can also be used to help enforce the internet rules. Discuss with your child who is going to be the person or persons who serve as the accountability person. Examples of internet rules:

- The use of smartphones and laptops is only permitted in common areas.
    - Charge phones in common areas
- Time for internet and smartphone use: 9am to 8pm
- Use the internet for constructive purposes
    - Use the internet to communicate with friends and people I know in real life

- Use the internet to help with homework and business matters
- Use the internet to assist me in learning about my passions
- Use the internet to help me with the artistic process
- 60 minutes of screen time a day is permitted.

Write down the rules and display them where everyone in the family can easily see them. Use the rules to teach your child self-discipline. Children push boundaries; that is their job. As your child's parent, it is your job to matter-of-factly hold your child accountable for their behavior. Pull your child back in bounds. Let your child know that you are teaching them to be successful.

Holding your child accountable means having consequences to apply if your child searches for and uses internet pornography at your house. Have consequences associated with breaking the internet rules. Here are some examples of consequences that can be applied if your child violates the internet rules and visits pornography websites:

- Talk with your child about what is going on
- Withhold the giving of some positive affirmations
- Decrease or remove one of your child's privileges
    - 60 minutes of screen time a day decreases to 45 minutes of screen time for 3 days
- The use of a family car can be only used for school and practice

- Decrease your child's earning from their chores

Notice the rules avoid the use of any "Do not." If your child can learn from rules that have positive statements, frame your rules in the positive. Some children may need clearer rules such as, "Do not visit pornography sites." For some parents, holding your child accountable for their compulsive pornography use is going to mean just talking to your child and help them process emotions regarding their continued use. Some parents will have to withhold incentives or privileges from their children because they will not learn another way. In this case, the child is forcing the parent to use a more restrictive form of consequence because they have not learned thus far.

Question from a parent. "How do I implement internet rules, if I have never had internet rules before?"

Response: Again, have a sit-down discussion with your family. If you pay for the internet and pay for services on their smartphone, then you have authority over the rules that are created around their use of your internet. Outside of that, you are their parent and children are to respect their parents. Further, when you provide housing for your child, inform your child that the internet rules are an extension of the house rules.

If your child does not consent to follow the rules and to only use a smartphone and laptop in common areas, then consider turning off their cell phone line and internet access until they are ready to consent to the terms and conditions that are outlined in the family's internet use agreement. If your child attempts to bully or harass you about the situation, then you have a bigger issue on your hands; if this is the case, consider seeking professional help immediately.

There is a difference between a natural push back on the implementation of internet rules, but this does not cross the line of being aggressive or intimidating. Suppose your child is attempting to intimidate you into letting them do whatever they want, consider talking with an emotionally-available family member, therapist, or another likewise professional to address the situation. Alternatively, you can drop the issue of internet accountability and wait until your child is of age and you no longer have to legally provide your child with housing. I am imagining this is for the minority of cases and the majority, your child naturally pushes back on the implementation of internet rules, yet does it tolerably.

Most children are not abusive in their approach to pushing back. Adolescents resisting accountability resulting from internet rules and online monitoring can learn to accept the terms and conditions of internet usage. Turning off your child's access to the internet on their smartphone and laptops or taking them away is a sure-fire way to have your child realize that they will be held accountable for their internet activity. Suppose your child forces you to turn off their access to the internet or revoke their phone; doing so will allow them to miss their access to the internet and it has the ability to teach your child to appreciate internet access in their home. For adolescents aged 15 or 16 and older, I am not advocating censoring their access to internet sites. I am suggesting that you consider monitoring their internet activity and respond accordingly to behaviors that both honor and violate the internet rules. Consider setting up a separate account for each child on each device. This will allow you to customize the features for each child in your home. Some adolescents aged 15 and older who are out of control probably will need a filter block. For adolescents 15 and older, if the monitoring and accountability approach works, then just monitor their activity and respond accordingly. If the monitoring approach does not work and your child has no reduction in their visits to pornography sites, consider using blocks and filters. This no-nonsense approach to parenting teaches your child to appreciate the online access that is available to them in their home when they are abiding by the family rules.

When your child moves out of your house, your child will have the option to use internet pornography, assuming that they have enough money to support themself independently. If your child moves out and then decides to use internet pornography, that is their choice. You did everything in your power to guide your child along a path that is conducive to their personal and professional success. With that alone, you can have peace of mind about whatever happens with your child's use of pornography. To have peace of mind around the situation, your child does not need to recover. Yes, recovery is obviously preferred; but, as long as you know you did everything that you could to set your child up for success in their recovery, then you have done what it takes to have peace of mind about the situation. Moreover, you are reading this kind of book, so you are doing what it takes to have peace of mind about your child's problematic use of internet pornography.

If your child "runs the show" or has somehow taken the upper hand, take back the upper hand. This is part of the responsibility of being a parent. It seems that parents have a responsibility to monitor their child's use of the internet. As it is the parents' money that is paying for online access, it seems that parents have a responsibility to their family and community to do their best to educate and guide their child toward both constructive and prosocial behaviors. By reading a book such as this one, you are demonstrating that you are a responsible parent, and you are willing to do what it takes to assist your child in overcoming their pornography dependency. You should feel good about yourself for finding this information and wanting to help your child.

Instilling values and providing direction to the youth is one of the most important jobs that we have in society. As conscious adults, it is our responsibility to raise and mentor the youth with values that sustain human happiness and equality on Earth. This book is designed to highlight and educate you on key topics that are needed for your child to recover from their addiction. This guide is specifically created for adults who have an adolescent who has problematic use of internet pornography. Here is a list of accountability software programs that can be used to monitor your child's use of the internet:

- Accountable2You
- Bark
- Covenant Eyes
- EverAccountable
- Net Nanny
- Router Limits

For further details on specific software programs, please visit ChristopherBueker.com for more information. If you can work it into your budget, use one of these software programs to be informed about what your child's internet use looks like. If you can afford the purchase of a yearly subscription to one of these services, do it. Being able to look at your child's online activity helps hold them accountable for their actions and helps keep them safe.

Hold Your Child Accountable

If you would like your child to be successful, hold your child accountable for their behaviors. Holding your child accountable for their behaviors is a crucial step in recovery. This is something you will have to formulate between your spouse, your child, and you. Come up with a game plan about what accountability looks like for your family unit. I offer suggestions and tips about how to hold your child accountable gently and compassionately, and at the same time, develop a customized strategy for your family. When you hold your child accountable for their behaviors, do it matter-of-factly. State the behavior. Avoid having a tone with your voice. Avoid expressing anger or upsetness. If your child's behavior of relapse upsets you, process your emotions before talking to your child about their use of internet pornography. If another caregiver can talk with your child more gently and compassionately, then allow them to have the talk. If you have a spouse, have a sit-down conversation with your family; your spouse does most of the talking, and you are there to provide emotional support.

If your spouse is better suited to lead the conversation about your child's pornography use, then your partner should read this book as well. When you hold your child accountable for their behaviors, there is no room for judgment in this process. If your child perceives that they are being judged or condemned for their use, your child will be inclined to experience more shame or guilt than what is necessary for them to modify their behavior. When an individual wants to recover from using drugs or pornography and they relapse, the individual generally experiences remorse, which results from a difference in their behavior and intention. This is why identifying and reinforcing values that are based on care, empathy, dignity, justice, and thriving is very important.

Reward Your Child for Appropriate Behavior

Reinforce your child for staying clean or making progress in their recovery. When your child stays clean of pornography use for say, one week, reward your child with something that they like. When your child honors the house and internet rules, present them with an incentive. Reinforcing your child for their appropriate behaviors will condition them to behave in a way that is aligned with recovery and success. While reinforcing your child for engaging in desired behaviors, teach them to internalize the behavior. When reinforcing your child for staying free of pornography use, teach them that the incentive that you are providing will not last forever and that they need to realize that doing desired behaviors (such as using the internet for constructive purposes) will help them experience success in their personal and professional life.

To reinforce your child's ability to adhere to recovery, figure out what your child likes, and strengthen the behavior of staying clean for your child. When you reinforce your child for using the internet constructively, make use of free and low-cost incentives that you can regularly apply. When your child is in initial recovery, apply their reward 100% of the time; this is *continuous reinforcement*, which means that a reward is applied every time the desired behavior occurs. When your child moves to maintenance recovery, change your schedule to intermittent reinforcement, which will occur about 50% of the time.

As with the Community Reinforcement Approach (CFA), your child can participate in what therapists call *activities sampling* to encourage them "to try out or renew various activities that might be, or once were, fun and rewarding to them." These activities include "involvement in a church, attendance of Twelve Step meetings or classes, participation in common interest clubs, visits to alcohol-free establishments, or participation in volunteer programs."[47]

Used by concerned family members and close friends, Community Reinforcement Approach and Family Training (CRAFT) is a behavioral therapy approach that teaches family members and friends how to interact with their loved one who is struggling with addiction. Community Reinforcement Approach utilizes operant conditioning techniques to assist the dependent loved one in learning how to reduce use, enroll in treatment, begin recovery, and start enjoying a healthier life. Further, CRAFT is a behavioral approach that teaches family members and friends to feel better and to motivate their

---

[47] Miller, W. R., Meyers, R. J., & Hiller-Sturmhöfel, S. (1999). The community-reinforcement approach. *Alcohol research & health: the journal of the National Institute on Alcohol Abuse and Alcoholism, 23*(2), 116-121.

loved ones to change their behavior. CRAFT teaches family members new ways to interact with their addicted loved one so that they can move towards treatment and recovery. The techniques are designed to:

- Help families move their loved one toward treatment
- Help reduce the loved one's use, regardless if they are in treatment yet
- Improve the lives of the concerned family members and close friends

CRAFT combines CFA with family training to give family members tools and tips to encourage their loved one to seek professional treatment; it also provides the family members with defenses against addiction's damaging effects on themselves.

The Community Reinforcement Approach and Family Training "is designed to increase the odds of the substance user who is refusing treatment to enter treatment, as well as improve the lives of the concerned family members."[48] CRAFT teaches skills on how to:

- Identify their loved one's triggers that lead to the use
- Positively communicate with their family member
- Use positive reinforcement strategies
- Reward non-using behavior

---

[48] Smith, J. E., Campos-Melady, M., & Meyers, R. J. (2009). CRA and CRAFT. *Journal of Behavior Analysis in Health, Sports, Fitness and Medicine, 2*(1), 4.

- Take care of oneself
- Encourage their addicted family member to consider getting professional help from a therapist

As stated, CRAFT is an approach that heavily relies on operant conditioning. Through its application, CRAFT creates an atmosphere conducive so the individual can experience natural consequences that originate from their harmful use of a drug or behavior and learn to accept help. CRAFT informs the principles, strategies, and practices described in this book.

Operant conditioning is a type of learning process through which the strength of the behavior is modified by reinforcement or punishment. In operant conditioning, rewards or incentives are applied to individual performing the desired behavior. Positive and negative reinforcement play a central role in the development and maintenance of an addiction. Some examples of rewards for staying clean:

- Give verbal praise
    - "Good job, [your child's name]."
    - "When you stay clean for the week, I am happy with the progress that you have made."
    - "[Your child's name], we liked how you did what you said you were going to."
    - "I like how you accomplished your goal this week."
    - "You have made a lot of progress so far. Keep it up!"

- Give your child a big hug
- Schedule quality time with your child
- Extend curfew for 30 or 45 minutes for the weekend
- Give your adolescent dating privileges
- Give your child a low-cost or no-cost (to your child) dance or music lesson
- Give access to a cell phone or more data
- Give car privileges or extra car time
- Allow your child to select the show/film
- Cook your child their favorite meal
- Plan a pizza night, allow your child to choose the toppings
- Allow your child to have a few friends over to spend the day or the night together
- When your child has all the clothes they need, buy them some new clothes that they like

Teach your child that you are rewarding them for honoring the house and internet rules; inform them that there will be a time when they live independently and that they will have to continue to be free from pornography use without receiving a reward. Teach your child to continue behaving appropriately because developing constructive habits will help them succeed in their personal and professional endeavors. Further, weigh different reinforcers and incentives that you apply to your child's behavior. That is, for the more expensive or more time-costly endeavors, apply these rewards on a less frequent basis and for larger accomplishments.

Question from a parent: "My child says that they do not like any of the free or low-cost activities that can be used to experience quality time or reward desirable behavior. How do I work on building my relationship with my child and reward them for clean behavior when they say that they do not enjoy any of the suggested activities?"

Response: Consider persuading your child to at least give it a try. Ask them what they would like to do. If you have not done it for some time, encourage your child to be open-minded about it. Let your child know that you value family time and emotional health; to live out those family values, spending quality time together is needed. If you can be gentle about it, let your child know that their desire not to want to engage in quality time is not serving their highest good. If your child wants to experience success in future relationships, let your child know that it is in their best interest to spend time together. Do it gently and lovingly; be sincere. After talking with your child, do not pressure them about it. Give your child a little bit of time to stew it over. In a week or so, bring the topic up again; ask your child to do one of the activities on the list or some they would like to do. Be persistent. Avoid being overbearing about it. Keep asking humbly. You can do it. Give your child space to feel your hearted-centeredness, and it all works out.

Surrender and Let Go

Surrender to something greater than your human ego. Let go of those things that do not serve you. Practice non-attachment. Often, people struggling with addiction believe that they can control their addiction or recover from their destructive use on their terms by fighting hard enough. The scientific literature simply does not support this view. Studies have found that recovery from substance addiction can take many treatment episodes to occur before the individual enters into maintenance and long-term recovery. Surrendering is crucial to the recovery process, both for the individual recovering and you as their parent. People struggling with addiction must acknowledge that they have a behavioral problem; they are best suited for recovery when they admit that they have little power over their addiction.

In my humble opinion, one cannot talk about recovery from addiction without mentioning Alcoholics Anonymous and the Twelve Steps program. As stated earlier in the book, addiction is about a lack of connection. The basis of the Twelve Steps fellowship is connection. Further, your child needs to surrender themselves to a person or a few people that can help them recover from their addiction. Willpower is not the key to recovery. Surrendering is the key to recovery. Telling someone struggling with an addiction to exercise more willpower over their addiction is like telling someone with a broken leg to walk it off. Letting go is being non-attached to the outcome of your child's addiction and recovery.

Take Action for Recovery

As you may know, your contentment and happiness come from within you, and regardless if your child recovers or not, you can have peace within. As a parent of a loved one, it is much easier to have peace within when you have dedicated some amount of time and energy to assist your child in overcoming their behavioral addiction. How much time and energy you give your child's problematic use is your choice. Simply, being okay with your child recovering and being okay with them continuing to struggle with problematic use of pornography puts your child and you in the best position for them to recover.

Your child also needs to surrender; but, for you to teach about non-attachment, you have to practice it yourself. If you are helping your child and you are putting a lot of energy into, "[Your child's name], you are going to recover. It will be much better when you do recover. I know you can do this. Do this recovery thing for me." It is a lot less likely to work that way. To increase the likelihood of achieving your preferred outcome, be non-attached to the outcome. Practice non-attachment; stay humble.

Non-attachment is another word for surrender. In popular culture, surrendering is often referred to as letting go. *Surrender* can be defined as giving oneself over to something bigger than the individual's ego. Surrendering is also key in Twelve Steps programs such as Alcoholics Anonymous and Narcotics Anonymous. In recovery, the choice to surrender to something bigger than the individual's ego may come from hitting rock bottom as in losing a job, losing an important relationship, getting into legal trouble, etc. You are reading this book because you would like to help your child raise their rock bottom. That is, to overcome the incredible power of addiction, your child needs to surrender themselves to something greater than their human ego.

In this chapter, you learned:

- The authoritative parenting approach allows you to guide and teach your child successfully so that they have the greatest likelihood of living their best life.
- Coping skills are constructive thought patterns and behaviors that allow an individual to relieve stress and avoid destructive behavior.
- For people struggling with addiction, triggers are environmental stimuli or emotional states that create an intense desire to use; teach your child to identify their triggers and use their coping skills.
- Identify your child's privileges. Identify desired behaviors. Create house and internet rules.
- When your child is honoring the internet rules, apply a reward; when they visit pornography websites, talk to your child, and consider removing a privilege.
- Be clear about your expectations of your child's behavior; be consistent with your application of incentives and privilege revocation. Use the least restrictive form of privilege removal.
- Authoritative parenting involves keeping your child safe by gently holding them accountable for their internet behaviors.

- If your child is younger, apply internet filters; censor pornography sites. When your child is approaching late adolescence, monitor their internet activity.
- Censoring your teenager may prevent them from accessing pornography while at your house; but this will not teach them how to use the internet for constructive purposes.
- Accountable 2 You, Bark Covenant Eyes, Ever Accountable, Net Nanny, and Router Limits are technology-based solutions that you can use to filter and monitor your child's internet activity.
- Hold your child accountable for their behaviors. Reinforce your child for doing the desired behavior.
- Community Reinforcement Approach and Family Training (CRAFT) is a behavioral therapy approach that teaches family members and friends how to interact with their loved one who is struggling with addiction.
- Surrendering to a power that is greater than the human ego is very important in recovery; letting go of being attached to an outcome increases the likelihood that the preferred outcome will happen.

Break Free of Chains

Chapter 6
Maintain Long-Term Recovery

For most people, recovery is a lifelong process. After sobriety has been maintained for a short while, the euphoria associated with early recovery subsides, and the recoveree is entering into maintenance recovery. This is a time in their life where they are adjusting to the benefits of clean living and can look forward to more of the positive benefits of recovery, as they maintain a state of being clean. Here is a summary of all the areas that you need to address to formulate your behavioral system:

- What are your child's motivators? What do they work for?
- What does your child like to do?
- What can we do together?
- What are our house rules?
- What are the internet rules?
- What are the rewards associated with following the rules?
- When my child avoids visiting pornography sites, what can I give them?
- What are the consequences associated with not following the rules?
- If my child visits pornography websites, am I going to remove a privilege? If so, for how long?
- Do I just talk to my child about why they are visiting pornography sites?

- Does my child need to attend a support group?
- Does my child need individual therapy?
- Do I need individual therapy?
- Will our family benefit from a Dialectical Behavior Therapy group?

As your child develops, the behavioral plan that you come up with for your child will be subject to change. What worked with one child does not always work with another child. Children and adults have different ways of learning. In summary, ask the aforementioned questions to your spouse and yourself to help put together an accountability program that works for your child. If another parent is present, of course, communicate with that person as well about how to proceed.

Some adolescents dependent on internet pornography can learn to abstain from its use simply by knowing that they are being monitored and that they will have to face Mom or Dad or both about the matter. For some adolescents, this will not work; they have to feel it to learn. These kinds of adolescents have a much stronger dependency or addiction to internet pornography. The kinds of adolescents still using pornography despite being monitored and held accountable for their behaviors need to have one of their privileges removed to learn that when they visit pornography sites, they will have less access to the internet or fewer or no car privileges, for example.

If you can teach your child to abstain from internet pornography use without removing their privileges, do that! More power to you. That is a great thing. This approach may be impractical for some families. I recommend you start here though. Start with: hold your child accountable for their use of internet pornography by simpling talking about how it happened. You say, "After checking the internet history and search words for the week, I noticed that you visited pornography sites more than one time." Ask:

- What is going on?
- How did that happen?
- What emotion were you feeling before you used pornography?
- After you used, what did it feel like?
- When you had the urge to use, did you think about using your coping skills?
- What are your coping skills?
- Did you ever have an urge this week where you used your coping skills and were able to avoid use?
- What was that like?

Asking open-ended questions is a great way to get a person talking; I know this from my personal and professional experience. If you are able to, help your child process their emotions. Hold space for your child. Love your child. Remember, your child is a reflection of you. Be gentle with your child.

Be Mindful of Substitute Addictions

Be aware that a person struggling with addiction may significantly reduce or abstain from the use of one behavior or substance and simultaneously develop compulsive use of another drug or behavior; from my clinical experience, the individual's newfound dependency is a little bit less severe yet ultimately, still detracts from the individual living their best life. That is, the individual's use of the new substance or process also causes negative impacts on the user's life. For example, growing up, two people that I know had anorexia during their adolescent years, and one of the persons appears to still struggle with body image. In the process of attempting to recover from her eating disorder, she also developed a work addiction. Further, many patients of mine who are in recovery from opioid dependency developed an addiction to pornography or emotional eating. Another widely used replacement behavior involves a psychological dependency on sugar. Addiction to sugar is way less dangerous than is an addiction to opiates, such as fentanyl; so, in the eyes of harm reduction, this switch is much celebrated.

The using individuals recover from one addiction, yet their dependency morphs into another behavior that they compulsively engage in. This is not uncommon for people in recovery because the root of their addiction is not taken care of. In the previous chapters, I talked about the importance of processing trauma and resolving past issues, especially when recovering from dependency problems.

Hemispheric bilateral stimulation such as in EMDR and the butterfly hug, Emotional Freedom Techniques, Trauma Releasing Exercises, Somatic experiencing, trauma-responsive therapy, Yoga, and meditation help get at the root cause of one's addiction. If the individual does not get at the root of that which was driving and sustaining the addiction, they will likely continue to struggle on an everyday basis. That is, the recovering person may be able to remain abstinent, but may still feel like it is a daily struggle to avoid use. Using is always on the individual's mind. It is an epic battle every day. I know, I have been there. This is an example of a person abstaining from use, but not getting to the root of their problem. That is, abstaining from the use itself is a worthwhile goal to achieve, but if the person never changes the other behaviors that exacerbated their use and turned their experimental use into compulsive and destructive use, the struggling individual will never really heal from that which ails them.

Alcoholics Anonymous, the largest and original Twelve Step fellowship program, calls this kind of person a *dry drunk*. As stated earlier in the book, a dry drunk never looks at the origin of their behavior and struggles on an everyday basis, yet they remain free of use. If you feel called to, you can encourage your child to get to the root of their addiction. Encourage your child to learn whatever it takes to learn or process whatever they need to process.

Positive Core Values

Emphasize value-centered living with your child. Instill values such as dignity and respect for all people, inclusion, equality, compassion, and fairness into your child. Live out these values. To increase the likelihood that your child recovers, ask yourself if there is anything to change about yourself. Core values are a description of our character, how we behave, or what we like. Core values guide our behaviors, decisions, and actions. An individual's core values are the foundation for decision-making and can inspire positive change. Core values are a powerful tool in living a life that is aligned with one's passions and purpose. Core values hold strong no matter what, they endure through the years. Not everyone has core values identified in their life. Establish your core values. Identifying your core values gives you a compass in which you navigate the world. One way to think about core values is that it is your line in the sand. It lets you know what you are willing to do and what you are not willing to do. Your core values can be likened to a GPS, they determine what you are comfortable doing and what you are not comfortable doing.

In my opinion, my values are the most important thing I will ever have. A value is something you think is more important than anything else. Values are what you consider to be more important than your feelings. For example, a person who uses a substance or uses internet pornography often feels like using. Then, there are the people who recover from their addictions, and they avoid succumbing to the desire to use. So, the question becomes, "What keeps the recovering person from using?" A value. In this case, the value is staying clean and healthy. This is one particular reason that values are so important in recovery.

Your child needs to ask themself: "Why am I interested in recovery?" Or is this something that is coming from your spouse or you? If this is the case, educate your child more. To educate your child and to get them to question why they engage in destructive behavior, consider emphasizing the values of self-care, healthy relationships, and positive self-esteem. Doing activities and exercises emphasizing values as such is a practical way of leading by example. Engaging in activities and outings as a family where communication is involved, and everyone has input will yield experiences where you can explore living out your core values. Give your child plenty of opportunities where they can accomplish things that allow them to feel good and boost their self-esteem. Further, educate your child about the benefits of volunteering. Associate volunteering with more job opportunities and economic success.

Helping your child identify their core values will significantly increase the likelihood of recovery from pornography addiction. If your child does not have their values identified, they are more likely to resist recovery; in other words, if your child has not identified that healthy relationships and success are important to them, your child may not want to recover from their behavioral addiction. When your child and you identify core values such as healthy relationships, accountability, and compassion, it will be much easier for your child to get behind their treatment and recovery. Here is a list of valucs:

- Accountability
- Achievement
- Adaptability
- Adventure
- Authenticity
- Autonomy, Independence

- Awareness
- Balance, Harmony
- Beauty
- Community
- Compassion, Kindness
- Conflict Resolution
- Contribution, Giving back
- Cooperation
- Courage
- Creativity
- Curiosity
- Determination
- Discipline
- Enthusiasm
- Excellence
- Fairness, Justice
- Faith
- Family, friendships, and healthy relationships
- Growth
- Happiness, Joy
- Health, Well-Being, Fitness
- Honesty, Openness, Transparency
- Humility

- Humor, Fun, Silliness
- Inner Peace
- Integrity
- Knowledge
- Leadership
- Learning
- Love
- Loyalty
- Meaningful work
- Optimism
- Peace
- Positive attitude
- Purity, Cleanliness
- Recognition
- Reliability
- Respect
- Responsibility
- Selfless service
- Spirituality, Religion, The Good Life
- Stability, Security, Safety
- Success
- Trustworthiness
- Truthfulness

- Wealth
- Wisdom

Pick 5 to 9 values and hone in on the first 5. If living your life based on values is a novel idea to you, start with 5 and focus on those 5. Live out those 5 values first. Then, expand from there; or start off with 3 values. Start off with a number that is not overwhelming for you. Healthy relationships are a foundational value for virtually all human beings. If you need to improve your ability to live out your value of healthy relationships, focus on building relationships first. When you work on living out your values, it significantly increases the likelihood that your child will also recover from their addiction. You change, and the world you experience changes. The only way to change the world we experience is by changing ourselves.

Identify your core values. If you need to, change your behaviors, so you can more fully live out your values. Remember, that you cannot control your child's behavior; you can only control your response to their behaviors. Hold space for your child. You can do it. You are this far already; showing up is more than fifty percent of the battle. Have faith and be persistent. It is not over. Life is always changing and evolving. Further, nothing is under control. Nothing is set in stone and you consciously create what you experience. Humans are interesting creatures and usually evolve; yet, in some cases, humans devolve; i.e., they form an addiction to a substance or unhealthy behavior. Conclusively, identify and live out core values, and you will increase protective factors that are conducive to a successful recovery from addiction.

Live for the Why

Live a purpose-driven life. It is in the nature of all humans to have something to look forward to, to give themselves a reason for getting up in the morning and experiencing all the ups and downs of life. No matter the reason, without having a purpose in life, a person will only wander through life without living life to the fullest. The first step in living a purpose-driven life involves establishing your core values. You will determine the way you set up your priorities, the way you behave, and how you make decisions. Your core values represent a unique set of principles that you intend to uphold, no matter the circumstances.

Find meaning in your life. Define your purpose in life. Your ultimate purpose in life can be to align with your core values. If your goals, values, and behaviors align, you significantly increase the likelihood that you experience contentment and happiness in your life. If your values and behaviors are not aligned with one another, you will not have what it takes to reach your goals. As humans, we need to be driven by something more than just simply achieving for the sake of achieving. If an individual's only value is the achievement in and of itself, they will not have what it takes to overcome obstacles that are present when making progress on the accomplishment of meaningful goals.

Find your passion. Pursuing your passion is one of the major things that will keep you motivated and help you achieve more success in each aspect of your life. Defining your passions will also guide you in creating an ideal work-life balance.

Become self-aware. To make sure that everything you do is in alignment with your ultimate purpose, you need to understand yourself better than anyone else. Identify your strengths and your limitations, your likes and dislikes, and you will significantly increase the likelihood that you will find the intention and motivation behind every action. Also, seek to understand why you behave the way you do. The self-aware person does not waste time with things that do not bring any positive contribution to their life; the conscious person dedicates their time and efforts to endeavors that are conducive to happy and successful living.

Emphasize Giving Back

Teach your child about the importance of contributing to their family and community. There is such power in any individual giving their time and energy to serve and contribute to the other. *Volunteering* is a "voluntary act of an individual or group freely giving time and labor for community service."[49] Volunteering can be seen as the underpinning of a community. Volunteering and giving back is about making connections. As addiction is about a lack of meaningful connection with oneself, others, nature, and a higher power, volunteering can be seen as part of the remedy for those struggling with addiction. When we step outside of thinking about ourselves, and we think about what we can do for others, we are entering into the territory of giving back, contributing, and volunteering. Further, there is no one way to give back.

---

[49] Wilson, J. (2000). Volunteering. *Annual review of sociology*, *26*(1), 215-240.

There are many ways of giving back and contributing to the greater good.

People are favorable to giving back and contributing to their community because they care about other people. It can be so easy for people to get into the routine of the daily grind, and that is why volunteering can be so important. It allows someone to break free of the challenges associated with everyday routine. Often enough, teens and adults alike turn to pornography because they are stressed out or frustrated with the situations that they face in their personal lives. Volunteering gives the individual a way to make a change for the good of society. Giving back and contributing to the greater good tends to bring out the best in people. When people contribute and give back, people truly care about the cause they are giving too, and at the same time, they also engage in volunteering because it makes them naturally feel good.

Volunteering can be part of your child's efforts in making amends. Making amends is viewed as the restitution that needs to take place to further cement the individual in their recovery. Making amends is the Eighth Step of the Twelve Step program; it says to make a list of all the persons we harmed throughout our addiction and become willing to make amends to them all. The Ninth Step says to make direct amends to such people, except when doing so would injure them or others. Volunteering is a great way to give back and make amends to the groups of people that are being harmed by the pornography industry.

As stated previously, the pornography industry creates much harm, especially to women and children. Individuals using pornography that sexualizes and degrades women bring harm and suffering into the world; in my humble opinion, using free tube-style internet pornography is not a victimless offense. As touched upon in the previous chapters, women endure much harm through their voluntary or involuntary involvement in the pornography industry; it would be challenging to make amends to the victims personally. Consider having your child give back to certain populations that are exploited by the pornography industry. Volunteering at an organization that serves women, children, and the indigent is a good way to make amends for bringing harm to the world. Serving at a soup kitchen is a great way to help your child clear their karma regarding their pornography use.

Continue to Intermittently Reinforce

If your child benefits from it, continue to intermittently reinforce them for staying clean. As mentioned in a previous chapter, in behaviorism, intermittent reinforcement is a conditioning schedule in which a reward or incentive is randomly applied; that is, the reward is not administered each time the desired behavior is performed. It differs from continuous reinforcement because the intermittent reinforcement schedule applies the incentive only some of the time on a randomized basis. For example, when your child stays clean for a week, apply the reward randomly and unpredictably. There is an increased likelihood that the desired response of staying clean will continue after the reward has been removed with intermittent reinforcement conditioning; further, the behavior of being abstinent lasts longer with intermittent reinforcement than if the reward was applied every time.

Intermittent reinforcement is when the reward is applied inconsistently and occasionally. Operant conditioning is a learning process in which new behaviors are acquired and modified due to the association and consequences of those behaviors. Reinforcing a behavior increases the likelihood it will occur again in the future. In operant conditioning, the scheduling of reinforcement is an important aspect of the learning process. When and how often we reinforce a behavior can have a dramatic impact on the strength and rate of the response.

Figure out a reinforcement schedule. When raising a child to be successful, having rules, and enforcing those rules is important. This is how accountability is connected to the application of the reward. Again, find out what your child likes so you can apply the reward when your child honors the rules. When your child is in early recovery, apply the reward 100% of the time. As they enter into long-term (maintenance) recovery, apply the reward about 50% of the time. It is as easy as flipping a coin. The rules you create are up to you. I offer some suggestions. With the input of your child, you will establish family and internet rules that serve your child's highest good. Write the rules down. Display them in a common area where each family member can view the rules. Once you have the rules established, you can determine if your child is following the rules and guidelines. When your child can stay free of use, you will apply the reward to your child, thus reinforcing your child's behavior of staying clean.

In this chapter, you learned:

- When your child is free of use for an extended period of time and is emotionally stable, your child is moving into maintenance recovery, which is sustained through looking at the larger picture.

- The questions you need to ask to formulate your behavioral system. Your rules, consequences, and privileges most likely will change over the years as your child develops and matures.

- What questions to ask when your child clearly visits pornography sites.

- Asking open-ended questions allows your child to feel more comfortable and to talk more freely about the topic.

- Often, individuals in recovery significantly reduce or eliminate the use of one chemical or behavior and then develop another habit that also contains drawbacks; i.e., the cigarette smoker who quits and then becomes addicted to food.

- Live a value-centered life. Identify your family's core values. Examine the things that are important in your life. Align your behaviors with your values. Define your purpose in life.

- Become more aware. Align your thoughts, words, and actions. Dedicate yourself to constructive activities that enhance your contentment and happiness. Teach your child to do the same.

- Emphasize the value of volunteering in the community. Volunteering allows your child to give back to the community.
- If your child continues to benefit from reinforcement, continue to intermittently apply the reward. Connect your verbal praise and other forms of reinforcement to internal mechanisms of reward such as feeling good and having friends.
- Teach your child to internalize constructive behavior.

Chapter 7
A Society Free from Addiction

A Commentary on Addiction Prevention

Ideally, we want to prevent addiction for all members of the society. This book has been written with the estimation that the ideal was not achieved, and addiction has occurred with a child of yours. It is okay. You are reading this kind of book. You have the power to experience a better life. We all have the power to consciously create the lives we lead. To change what is out there, we need to change what is within. You are doing it!

Parent with the End Goal in Mind

Think about the end goal of parenting. How do I get there? Parenting with the end goal in mind is about raising children that are productive, happy, compassionate, creative, and living their best life. Parenting with the end goal in mind is about motivating, inspiring, and empowering children to design, create, and live their best lives. The mission of great parenting is to raise independent, capable individuals who have self-esteem and self-confidence; to raise children who are resilient and determined. Further, the question becomes, "What do I need to do as a parent to give my child the best chances of living their best life?"

Start addiction prevention from an early age. In age-appropriate language, teach your child from a young age about how there are good things and bad things on the internet. Encourage your child to follow rules that are designed to teach them how to be successful. Teach your child to be discerning and to think for themselves.

One of the keys to preventing addiction involves talking to your child in age-appropriate language about the internet, sex, drug use, and pornography from an early age. Obviously, youngsters do not need to know all of the specific and graphic details about adult topics. At the same time, children and adolescents need to receive the message that they need to follow the rules because it keeps them safe. Having age-appropriate rules is one of the best things you can do as a parent to help your child live an addiction-free life. Having equitable rules that are in the best interest of your child gives them the best chance for success in their personal and economic affairs. Having and following through with appropriate rules allows your child to feel safe and to explore their environment. Explaining the rules helps children learn and understand why it is in their best interest to follow the rules. Children need to know that the internet has good and bad things on it. As implied in the text, teach the child to internalize the meaning and spirit of the rule.

Teach and educate your child from an early age. Teach and educate your child that core values and having a structure allows a person to make choices that will lead to success. Having no structure leads to chaos, and not having enough flexibility leads to rigidity and possibly resentment toward that parent or caregiver. In parenting, it is a delicate balance between maintaining the structure and allowing things to flow freely. This balance and dance are different for different families. Try out various techniques and see which ones are best suited for your family. Create age-appropriate rules. The following are elements that help you establish which rules are going to be right for your child. Create and enforce house rules that orient:

- Clarity: Be clear when you set rules, privileges, limitations, and boundaries on your child's behavior.

- Consistency: Be consistent in enforcing the rules that you establish for your household. Consistently apply consequences that have been established for the broken rule.

- Flexibility: As your child grows, they will be ready for additional privileges and changes in the rules and the limits.

- Communication: Frequently talk about privileges, rules, and limitations. At any time, be willing to discuss the fairness of a rule and the reasons for it.

- Emotions: Assist your child with learning to talk about their feelings. Model this behavior by giving your child a vocabulary that allows them to express emotions. Do not shame or guilt your child for having emotions or expressing their emotions. Validate what your child is experiencing.

- Compassion: When your child breaks the rules, use encouragement and support.

- Incentives: Verbally reinforce your child. Praise your child when they follow the family rules, especially when your child does what is expected of them without reminders from your spouse or you.

Instill a sense of social responsibility in your child. Let your child know that you expect them to behave morally, honestly, and fairly. When creating your household rules, promote your child's sense of self-respect and self-esteem. Raising a child that is self-sufficient, kind, and productive does not come from good luck. It comes about by providing structure and boundaries for your child to play and learn in. Creating safe boundaries for the adolescent helps the youth feel safe in their exploration.

Create a culture based on humanistic values

Society needs to create a culture that values civil liberties. Society needs leaders in society to embrace and live out likewise values. Some of the humanistic values that, when adopted on a large scale, will benefit society include:

- Respect for diversity
- Inclusion
- Equality
- Compassion
- Individual liberty
- Social responsibility
- Work-life balance
- Ideas over things
- Feedback and growth
- Engagement and purpose

These kinds of values need to be adopted by our culture in order for society to experience widespread freedom from addiction. It seems to me that conscious individuals are responsible for living out these values in our everyday lives. If a person wants society to change, they have to change themselves. The whole can only change when the individual parts within the whole change. Meaning, all individuals have a responsibility to play in contributing to a society that is free of addiction.

Question: "How do we live out these kinds of values?"

Response: Live in your heart center. Treat other people and yourself with compassion. Be a kind person in all situations. The world you experience is a reflection of your inner reality. As above, so below. That which is happening on the inside is reflected out into the external world. That is why your child can learn to recover from their problematic use of pornography. Your child's addiction took root, so they can learn to recover from it. However, your child will have to be determined. We all have a choice in these kinds of matters.

Further, a person never goes wrong when they take action from a place of compassion. There are many paths to liberation, yet none of them cross through violence. That is, compassion and non-harming is the common thread among all bonafide world religions, life philosophies, and spiritual paths. Conclusively, live in your heart center, and you are helping to bring about the new consciousness that is emerging on Earth.

Unfortunately, there is a long history of men dominating women. The modern pornography industry and sex trafficking is the most henious and violent expression of patriarchal society. In the previous chapters, I talked about the harms associated with the pornography

A Society Free from Addiction

industry. In this chapter, I talk about what needs to be done to ensure equality for all human beings.

Now, I yield to the wisdom of intellectual heavyweight Noam Chomsky about how to address the injustices associated with the pornography industry. When Chomsky was asked about his stance on pornography, he stated that "Pornography is humiliation and degradation of women. It's a disgraceful activity. Just take a look at the pictures. I mean, women are degraded as vulgar sex objects. That's not what human beings are."

Interviewer: "But didn't the [female] performers choose to do the job and get paid?"

Chomsky: "The fact that people agree to it and are paid, is about as convincing as the fact that we should be in favor of sweatshops in China, where women are locked into a factory and work fifteen hours a day, and then the factory burns down and they all die. Yeah, they were paid and they consented, but it doesn't make me in favor of it, so that argument we can't even talk about."

Interviewer: "How should we improve the production conditions of pornography?"

Chomsky: "By eliminating degradation of women, that would improve it. Just like child abuse, you don't want to make it better child abuse, you want to stop child abuse. Suppose there's a starving child in the slums, and you say 'well, I'll give you food, if you'll let me abuse you.' Well, there happen to be laws against child abuse, fortunately. But suppose someone were to give you an argument. Well, you know, after all a child's starving otherwise, so you're taking away their chance to get some food if you ban abuse. I mean, is that an argument? The answer to that is to stop the conditions in which the child is starving, and the same is true here. Eliminate the conditions in which women can't get decent jobs, not permit abusive and destructive behavior."[50]

As Chomsky stated, eliminate the conditions that make pornography and other forms of sex trafficking alluring to women. We need to create a society where all people have the opportunity to grow and prosper. We need to create a society where the feminine is honored. We need to create a society where people of all sexes and genders are empowered to live their fullest life. People of all walks of life are equal, and the modern pornography industry produces material that conditions people, especially young people to think otherwise. As Martin Luther King stated, "Injustice anywhere is a threat to justice everywhere."[51]

Societal Freedom from Addiction

Imagine a society where people are in the process of achieving their highest good. Imagine a world where people are happy and free. Imagine a world where people have opportunities to live their best life. I can see a world where all the people and beings are happy and free. I see a society of happy children and content adults. I see a world where a large majority of the people are living their best life. In this kind of world, people pursue their passions

---

[50] Chomsky, N. (2008). Noam Chomsky on Pornography. Retrieved 2020, from
https://www.youtube.com/watch?v=SNlRoaFTHuE&t=13s
[51] King Jr, M. L. (1992). Letter from Birmingham jail. UC Davis L. Rev., 26, 835.

and are successful in life. Right now, humanity is entering into our post-competition era, where humanity realizes that all life is connected and that creation is the key to wealth, not competition. I see a society that is healthy and free. What do you see? Will you help dream up this kind of free and compassionate world?

In this chapter, you learned:

- Parenting with the end goal in mind helps you raise your child that gives them the best opportunity to experience success in life.
- Having ongoing talks about sex, drugs, and pornography and listening to your child's concerns increases the likelihood that they will decide to make safe choices.
- Teach your child from a young age. Conversations about sex, drugs, and pornography need to occur on an ongoing basis. Have ongoing conversations with your child; be more concrete and candid about the topic, as your adolescent develops and matures.
- Create rules that are clear and consistent. Be flexible; also look at the spirit of the rule. As you apply consequences, be compassionate. Instill a sense of social responsibility in your child.
- As a society, we need to create a culture based on equality, compassion, inclusion, intrapersonal growth, and liberty; this will help us create a society that is free of addiction.

- By being compassionate to yourself and all other people, you help create a culture that is based on equal rights, justice, and freedom.
- As stated by Noam Chomsky, society needs to eliminate both the degradation of women and the conditions in which women are unable to secure decent jobs.
- We need to create a society where people of all sexes and genders are empowered to live their best life.

www.ingramcontent.com/pod-product-compliance
Lightning Source LLC
Chambersburg PA
CBHW072155100526
44589CB00015B/2240